Speaking both to the wider
Strange and Mike Ovey c
and embarrassed approaches ~~to the Bible, and provoke us~~
to a greater confidence in this amazing God-given gift to
humanity.

Steve Clifford,
General Director, Evangelical Alliance, U.K.

At a time of increasing pressure on the Christian community,
here's a great book to insert vertebra into our elastic spine! In
an accessible but robust way, it strengthens our confidence
in Scripture, builds a compelling apologetic for our
conversations with non-Christians, and urges us to follow
Jesus' example by living wholeheartedly by that transforming
Word. I warmly commend it.

Jonathan Lamb,
CEO and Minister-at-Large, Keswick Ministries

What a super book! The shocking reality is that many
Christians are as ashamed of the Bible as they are of that
eccentric uncle they have to invite to the wedding! He is
loved and understood within the family, but is certainly not
for public consumption. You will find this book, intellectually
satisfying, spiritually edifying and a most useful addition to
your apologetic tool bag. It is presented in easily digestible
portions, but will add to both your knowledge and your
confidence in using the Bible. I have already used many of
the arguments unpacked in the book. It is highly satisfying ...
the old uncle is not as he seems, he can still 'pack a punch'!

David Meredith,
Minister, Smithton Free Church of Scotland, Inverness

The great thing about this book is the way it deals with the
difficulties of belief in the Bible as the Word of God as a set
of highly *contemporary* issues, some quite subtle but all
highly important. The classic doctrines of revelation and
authority are carefully restated to answer and deconstruct

modern concerns and biases. I appreciated the way it made me think more clearly about this and challenged me to submit Christ more fully. There isn't anything quite like it.

Julian Hardyman,
Senior Pastor, Eden Baptist Church, Cambridge

In this engagingly written and pastorally sensitive book, barriers to engaging the Bible seriously are gently but effectively dismantled and current challenges to biblical authority and relevance are convincingly answered. Do you have a friend who can't understand why you appeal to the Bible for the truth about God and how to live in God's world? Give them this book. Are you troubled by the arguments mounted, even by some within the churches, against the reliability of the Bible and the truthfulness of its teaching? Read this book. Strange and Ovey understand the Bible but they understand us and the things that trouble us as well. The end result — well-founded, generous-hearted confidence.

Mark D Thompson,
Principal, Moore Theological College, Sydney

CONFIDENT

WHY WE CAN TRUST THE BIBLE

DANIEL STRANGE & MICHAEL OVEY

CHRISTIAN
FOCUS

Unless otherwise stated, Scripture quotations taken from the *The Holy Bible, New International Version®*, NIV® Copyright © 1973, 1978, 1984, 2011 by Biblica, Inc.® Used by permission. All rights reserved worldwide.

A CIP catalogue record for this book is available from the British Library.

Daniel Strange is the Academic Vice Principal at Oak Hill Theological College in London. He lectures on Culture, Religion and Public Theology. Dan is married to Elly and they have seven children. He is an elder at East Finchley Baptist Church.

Michael Ovey is the Principal of Oak Hill Theological College in London and teaches on Doctrine, Apologetics and Liturgy. He is married to Heather, and they have three children.

Copyright © Daniel Strange and Mike Ovey 2015

paperback ISBN 978-1-78191-554-7
epub ISBN 978-1-78191-571-4
Mobi ISBN 978-1-78191-572-1

10 9 8 7 6 5 4 3 2 1

Printed in 2015
by
Christian Focus Publications Ltd,
Geanies House, Fearn, Ross-shire,
IV20 1TW, Scotland, U.K.

www.christianfocus.com

Cover design by Daniel van Straaten

Printed and bound by Bell and Bain, Glasgow

CONTENTS

Last eve I paused beside the blacksmith's door,
And heard the anvil ring the vesper chime;
Then looking in, I saw upon the floor,
Old hammers, worn with beating years of time.

'How many anvils have you had?' said I,
'To wear and batter all these hammers so?'
'Just one,' said he, and then with twinkling eye,
'The anvil wears the hammers out, you know.'

And so, I thought, the Anvil of God's Word
For ages skeptic blows have beat upon;
Yet, though the noise of falling blows was heard,
The Anvil is unchanged, the hammers gone.

John Clifford

All people are like grass,
and all their glory is like the flowers of the field;
the grass withers and the flowers fall,
but the word of the Lord endures forever

1 Peter 1:24-25a

INTRODUCTION:

Have Confidence!

The great preacher C.H. Spurgeon might question the point of writing this little book. At a speech made at the Annual Meeting of the British and Foreign Bible Society, May 5th 1875, he uttered the following words:

> I think the time has gone for defending the Bible against anybody, whoever they may be—whether they happen to be a bishop, or to come from the opposite side. Wherever they may happen to come from, let them come! The Bible has been so often defended, and the defences are so admirable, that any more outworks would almost seem to be superfluous. I look upon the Bible now as the other day I did upon a little village church which I came across in the middle of a wood – Oakwood Chapel, in Surrey – a church subjected to a great many slips of the soil, or inclemencies of weather, and therefore buttressed until there are about twice as many bricks in the buttresses as there are in the church. There seems to me to have been twice as

much done in some ages in defending the Bible as in expounding it, but if the whole of our strength shall henceforth go to the exposition and spreading of it, we may leave it pretty much to defend itself. I do not know whether you see that lion—it is very distinctly before my eyes; a number of persons advance to attack him, while a host of us would defend the grand old monarch, the British Lion, with all our strength. Many suggestions are made and much advice is offered. This weapon is recommended, and the other. Pardon me if I offer a quiet suggestion. Open the door and let the lion out; he will take care of himself. Why, they are gone! He no sooner goes forth in his strength than his assailants flee. The way to meet infidelity is to spread the Bible. The answer to every objection against the Bible is the Bible.

So 119 years later are we being disrespectful in not taking the great man up on his 'quiet suggestion'? Do we disagree with his argument that it is in expounding the Bible that we defend Scripture? Are we defending and protecting the Lion unnecessarily? Should we be doing better things with our time?

Before we go any further, let's be very clear on this. Both authors of this book wholeheartedly agree that what gets us up in the morning is to bring people to sit under God's written revelation, reading it, wrestling with it, hearing it expounded, hearing it proclaimed, meeting the Lord Jesus in it. We know where the power is. We know where we are to find the real, authentic and life-giving Jesus.

But how do we get people plugged in? How do we make proper introductions? How might we poke our non-Christian friends into showing any interest in opening a Bible. And of course it's not just non-Christians. How do we help Christians (it might even be you!) who have lost confidence in the Bible? They have got lots of questions about the authority of the Bible and how this relates to Jesus' authority on our lives. They've been told that at the end of day, Jesus's opinion on various matters will sometimes trump other parts of the Bible.

This little book is aimed to give some help in this area. It's not meant as a substitute for reading, expounding and proclaiming the message of Scripture, or even to replace letting the Bible speak for itself from itself. Rather, in writing this book we simply recognise that, at the moment, our culture creates a certain distance and various barriers that make first contact, and indeed ongoing contact, quite difficult.

This is a book of two halves. The first half we've called, 'A Word for Them.' It's more outward-facing in trying to give some practical tips and suggestions in our conversations with non-Christians about the Bible. These tips are not meant to be very heavy or detailed (of course there are lots of resources we can point you to which are), but are simply meant to be possible ways for the 'average-normal-Christian' talking to your 'average-normal-non-Christian'. There are a number of bite-size chapters on issues of authority, culture, and the style, impact, and content of the Bible.

But that's only the first half.

The second half of our little book is called, 'A Word for Us.' This part is more inwardly facing. What does that mean?

We draw upon the discipline known as 'apologetics', which means applying biblical truth to unbelief; it is

all about giving a reason for the hope that we have
(1 Pet. 3:15). If we ever think about apologetics, perhaps
we think its focus is solely on non-Christians. In reality
though, apologetics is equally for Christians as well,
protecting us from unbelief, assuring us and strengthening
our faith.

Let's face some uncomfortable facts: many Christians
can struggle with exactly the same issues about the Bible
as their non-Christian friends. These are probably not
issues of complete biblical illiteracy (although very many
issues could be cleared up if we just had both a broader
and deeper grasp of biblical truth!). Rather we're talking
about questions and problems we have about the
Bible as we read the same blogs, and watch the same
documentaries as our non-Christian friends. We don't
live in a bubble. We all breathe the same cultural air. Over
time, we can start to harbour nagging doubts about the
Bible's ultimate authority, its total trustworthiness, its
contemporary relevance. We can start to lose confidence
not only in the Bible but in its divine author. Is God in
control? Can he be trusted? Is he moral? Does he care
and can he speak into my life and my struggles?

What's even worse, and very worrying, is that there
are plenty of recent examples of leaders within the
Christian community who are subjecting the Bible to
the same criticisms as those from without. However
well-intentioned they might be, they question whether
the historic view of the Bible – that Christians have held
over the centuries – might in our culture actually be
a barrier to belief, and particularly a barrier to getting
to know the real Jesus. They say that this historic view
is what could drive people away from faith. All this can

be very unsettling and unnerving. It's also very sad, in a tragic and ironic sort of way, because Christian leaders are not appointed by God to undermine confidence in the Bible, but to increase it.

Therefore, while the first half of our book is focused primarily on defending the Bible from the critics from *without*, the second half of our book is going to address issues brought up by the critics from *within*. Here we'll be looking at the authority of the Bible in the context of other authorities we have: Jesus's teaching on the difference between words of God and words of man; and Jesus' own defence and use of the Bible.

You will discover that the chapters in Part 2 are a little more meaty in content—they need to be, given the issues at stake. In both parts, you will also find some 'Going Deeper' sections which go into more detail on a particular concept and issue.

At the end of each chapter we've added some questions for you to think about. We hope the chapters are small enough for you to take one at a time and work through them either individually or in a small group.

Overall, our hope and our prayers are for men, women and children to have complete confidence in the Bible, so that they open the door and let the lion out.

Dan and Mike
August 2014

PART ONE:

A Word for Them

Where does the Bible fit into the life and times of our non-Christian friends, family and acquaintances?

While it's still fresh in the memory, please indulge us a little as we continue with Spurgeon's famous big cat illustration that opened up our book. Last year one of us took our kids to the 'Lions of the Serengeti' enclosure at Whipsnade Zoo. As the blurb says, 'our innovative viewing area offers uninterrupted views of our pride roaming the plains of Whipsnade, through three metre high floor to ceiling viewing windows.' It was an impressive view (although the lions didn't particularly want to 'perform' that day), but the glass was so thick that the experience was a little desensitising and quite frankly, tame (pardon the pun). You knew you were still in Dunstable, England and not in the Serengeti, Africa.

Not to worry though (I'm being sarcastic now!), because on our side of the glass was a 'real' lovely old lady, a zoo volunteer, who had on a table in front of her a 'real' lion pelt, and a 'real' lion skull, that the kids could handle and play with. Are you getting our point?

Key Summary

When it comes to the Bible, how do we get into a position where we can 'open the door and let the lion out'—a real, majestic, terrifying lion that is, and not some flea-bitten relic of a lion. We want to release the lion (who, by the way, is ready and waiting to be introduced). But there seem to be these big, thick, impenetrable walls in the way—which means that people's only 'experience' of the lion is rather uninspiring and, frankly, dead. *How do we break down these walls?*

The first part of our little book deals with what makes up the seemingly impenetrable walls. The walls range over a number of common problems that people have with regard to the Bible:

- problems of illiteracy and implausibility
- problems of culture and relevance
- problems of basic comprehension

1

Keeping it Real ... and Realistic

Introduction

We've started thinking about those walls that can separate people from engaging with the Bible. Now, of course, you might be someone who engages with people in everyday life who don't seem to have any walls—or only tissue-paper thin ones, which are easily ripped down. In your experience, these people are quite happy to engage with the Bible and the claims it makes. Praise God if this is you. Please get on with your let-the-lion-loose mission.

For many others, including ourselves among those 'others', the walls do seem very thick indeed! We don't think that this thickness is down to a lack of faith on our part about the power of God's Word, or the power of the Holy Spirit. There is certainly no desire on our part to dilute the Bible's message to make it more acceptable and palatable, muzzling the lion to domesticate it, as it were. The reality and thickness of the walls exist like any other barrier to unbelief, and we knock down those barriers with a healthy dose of prayer, proclamation and persuasion.

Up against the walls

When it comes to barriers to the Bible, what are these walls made out of? There are at least two factors we want to get out into the open as we start. One is ignorance, and another is implausibility. Let us explain.

1. The wall of ignorance

First, there's the wall of ignorance. We know, don't we, that not a year goes by without some new survey or poll highlighting new levels of biblical illiteracy. As Boyd Tonkin wrote a couple of years ago in *The Independent*, on the anniversary of the King James Bible,

> For anyone religious or not, who cares about the continuity of culture and understanding, Gordon Campbell lets slip a remark to freeze the blood. A professor at Leicester University, he recalls that 'When the name of Moses came up at the seminar I was leading, no one had any idea whom he might have been, though a Muslim student eventually asked if he was the same person as Musa in the Qur'an (which he is).'[1]

Wow! What a state we're in.

Now one might be tempted to think that such cultural ignorance is bliss. Doesn't this illiteracy give us a clean slate with people to tell them about the Bible? Well possibly, if our communication about the Bible

---

1   Boyd Tonkin, 'Battles of a Book', *The Independent* (December 31, 2010), http://www.independent.co.uk/arts-entertainment/books/features/battles-of-a-book-the-king-james-bibles-history-of-dissent-and-inspiration-2171902.html.

presumes such illiteracy and ignorance and we start with basic building blocks and work up from there. But in our conversations with non-Christians don't we simply presume too much knowledge? We basically think that people know what the Bible is, how it functions and what it says because we do and our Christian friends do. But your average guy today just doesn't, and as a result communication and comprehension become very difficult. One might say it's a Christian version of what communication gurus call 'The Curse of Knowledge': 'We start to forget what it's like not to know what we know'.[2] We see it happening a lot between doctors and their patients, and lawyers and their clients. I think we see it many times in our conversations about the Bible.

Let's do a little thought experiment. Taking the above example at Leicester University, how much would you have to back-track to explain to someone who Moses is starting with nothing? Do it now.

Breaking through the wall of biblical illiteracy, or rather chipping away at it, means being able to communicate from where people are, presuming nothing and explaining everything. Let's not be ignorant about our ignorance!

In terms of our attitude and character, it means being convinced and convicted of Ecclesiastes 7:10: 'Do not say, "Why were the old days better than these?" For it is not wise to ask such questions.' Yes, we can go dewy-eyed, be wistful, even self-flagellate, remembering a time when people knew what the Bible is, what it contains, what the Old Testament is, what a prophet is, who Moses is, how

---

2   Chip and Dan Heath, *Made to Stick* (London: Arrow, 2008), p. 46.

Moses points to Christ and so on. But in the phrase of our American colleagues here at Oak Hill College, 'We are where we are.' We can and should pray for elements of that time to return, but for now those times are not our times. There's a whole lot of unlearning that's gone on for well over a century between Spurgeon's times and ours. The slow chip, chip, chip will require empathy, patience, long-suffering and determination. Biblically speaking, it will mean suffering fools gladly without ourselves succumbing to that ugly vice that the Bible calls 'vain conceit'.[3]

In terms of our practice, breaking through this wall of biblical illiteracy might mean having to scale back and be more realistic when it comes to the aims and objectives of our conversations, our preaching and teaching about the Bible. We might be thinking every time: 'At the end of our chat about the Bible, I want people to know what the Bible is, what it's for, to whom it testifies, and then I want said person to confess that Jesus Christ is Lord, and to acknowledge that the Bible is God's Word: authoritative, sufficient, perspicuous, and necessary.' Instead of this it might be: 'At the end of the chat about the Bible, I want said person to go home, rummage around bookcases and boxes of detritus and find a copy of the Bible he or she was given x years ago and have a quick look at it and put it on the kitchen table.' It might mean thinking: 'At the end of talking about the Bible, I want said person to go home and set up to record the Channel 4 documentary on the Bible that was going to be on next week.' It might just mean, 'At the end of our

---

3   Phil. 2:3; Gal. 5:26.

chat about the Bible, I want people to google the word "Bible" on their phones and see what comes up.' Now of course the ultimate aim that we are always working towards in an intentional way, is for people to know what the Bible is, what it's for, who it testifies to and to confess that Jesus Christ is Lord, acknowledging that the Bible is God's word: authoritative, sufficient, perspicuous, and necessary. But we might have to work up to it slowly, a bit like introducing a baby to solids from liquids. It can be painfully slow (and very messy) from bland puree, to very small pieces, to slightly less small pieces, but at least you've got a chance of getting something into the vicinity of the mouth. Going straight in, even 'choo-choo-train style', with a pork chop is unrealistic, and probably will result in choking.

So let's be patient, take our time, move from step to step, play the long game and pray.

2. The wall of implausibility

Second, there's the wall of implausibility. When we talk about implausibility (and of course its reverse 'plausibility'), we're talking about those deeply embedded beliefs about stuff that are so deep we don't even ask if they are true or not. We just assume they are. It's these kinds of beliefs (or unbeliefs) that provide the background and structure that makes arguments easier or harder to understand and accept. These structures are a bit like an atmosphere—the cultural air that we breath. We take it for granted and it becomes just normal. We don't think about the beliefs, let alone question them.

In writing this book, we don't think we're being too controversial when we say that there is a deep implausibility about the Bible in our culture today. People, who might never have picked up a Bible in their lives, simply assume a whole load of negative things about it because since they were born they have been breathing in air that has told them and moulded them into believing that the Bible is … (fill in the missing word).

Implausibility, however, is maybe something we Christians have less patience with than ignorance. There's a sense in which we might go easier on those who are ignorant about the Bible, but are less forgiving with those who think the Bible and its claims are implausible.

If we want to talk about the 'plausibility' or 'implausibility' of a Christian truth within culture, it doesn't mean we're going theologically squidgy. It doesn't mean an obsequious 'cap in hand' pandering to the world, or a desperate prettifying of ugly reality. It certainly does not mean a denial of the sovereign work and power of the Holy Spirit, who is ultimately responsible not only for making dead hearts beat again but, more particularly, actually convincing us that God's Word is exactly that.

Talking about plausibility or implausibility, rather, is about being prayerfully aware and savvy about the form that unbelief takes in any given culture. It's about the way that humans collectively manifest all the wilful suppression and substitution stuff that Paul in Romans 1 talks about in such stark terms. It's seeing sociology and specifically the sociology of knowledge (yes, this is a real discipline that people think about!) as a tool we can use for rigorously Christian theological ends. It's about asking both why people don't believe and how people don't believe. Of course at rock bottom the root of disbelief is sin, but we can and need to set this out in more explanatory detail. To talk about plausibility or implausibility is relevant, wise and sound. When it comes to people taking the Bible seriously today, the glass wall of implausibility might seem impenetrable and impregnable. There are just so many issues that people have with the Bible in terms of its authority, relevance, morality, reliability and so forth.

When we take the time to consider why people think the Bible implausible, however, we'll be in a much better position to make right diagnoses and give appropriate treatment in the appropriate areas. We'll be able to give answers that are more scalpel-like and less like using a machete.

So let's pause to reflect on the specifics of people's unbelief; about their distrust and disdain of the Bible. Let's be patient, take our time, move from step to step, play the long game and pray.

Questions

1. There's an old saying in English law 'Ignorance of the law is no defence'. That suggests we should take ignorance of the law really quite seriously. But how seriously do you think we take ignorance of the Bible and its contents? How seriously should we take the ignorance of the Bible in Christians of our generation? Please read 2 Kings 22:1–23:27 and think through or discuss the following questions:

   • How seriously does Josiah treat his and his people's ignorance of God's law?

   • What is their response?

- How does God treat the ignorance of the kingdom of Judah?

2. We've stressed the way that our time is ignorant about the Bible and finds it implausible. Think of a friend or relative who is not a Christian:

   - What do they think the story of the Bible is?

   - What makes the Bible implausible to them? What are good ways of responding to those ideas of implausibility?

   - Check out with that friend or relative that you have understood them correctly about what they think the Bible's story is and why they find it implausible. Have you understood them correctly?

2

The Reasonableness of Revelation

Introduction

There's a big debate that carries on between academics, and in particular sociologists of religion, about whether the world is becoming less religious or more religious and how the U.K. fits into worldwide trends. It's been going on for decades. Many of us are probably unaware about this debate and its see-saw nature, apart from the occasional time in the media when there's a survey or a census, or some prominent public figure pronounces something provocative on a religious topic. Then Professor such and such is wheeled out into the daylight for a twenty-second soundbite, and then there's the usual round of radio phone-ins with titles like 'Are we losing our religion?' and 'Is God dead?' Then after a day or so things just seem to carry on as normal.

While we might not be able to feel it, little cultural shifts are happening all the time. It's a massive gut-feeling generalisation, but in terms of public perception and consciousness, maybe, just maybe, we might be 'doing God' a little more than we did in 2003.[1] (Sorry if you're outraged and want to contest this statement: you can't phone in!) Now, don't get excited, We're not talking revival, or that God is the new essential fashion accessory for this season, but that perhaps there is a little more toleration around, even in some media streams, about faith and belief. Of course it goes without saying that it can be faith and belief in anything.

However, if God, gods, 'something up there,' 'something out there,' 'something in here,' faith, spirituality, can be more easily broached in polite company, throwing in the word 'Bible' can still be guaranteed to give us an uncomfortable tumbleweed moment. There can be a number of reactions, all of which don't promote further conversation: wide eyes ('you can't be serious'); rolled eyes ('here she goes again'); glazed eyes ('what am I going to have for dinner tonight?').

Spiritual, yes. Bible, no. God or gods, maybe, Bible no. Whatever the reasons, when it comes to the Bible, implausibility and incredulity seem to go into over-drive.

Maybe one way to start chipping away at our wall of implausibility is to try to show that the whole idea of the Bible is not far-fetched but actually rather sensible, really. In order to do this, I would suggest that we don't start with the Bible, but with what the Bible claims to be: a self-communication from a personal God. If we start here, then we can work back to the Bible. Let's take it step by step.

---

1   I'm talking here about spin-doctor Alistair Campbell's infamous interjection, 'We don't do God,' to a journalist who wanted to question Tony Blair about his Christian faith.

Although we'll be talking about it in more
on, we need to start by talking about the gene
authority and trust.

1. You've gotta trust someone ... trust me!

Authority: we can't live with it, we can't live without it.

The radio phone-in, in fact, is a great example of what we think about authority. Even though there might be our old friend the professor back in the radio studio to give his professional opinion, a central idea underlying these shows is that really everyone's say is as valid as everyone else's. In a sense we're all experts and pundits and asked to give our opinion because 'damn it, we have the right to give it in our free democracy!'

One doesn't have to be a cultural guru to see that part of what's going on here is that there seems to be a deep suspicion of authority and authority figures, be it parents, teachers, police, politicians, priests and pastors. And we know, don't we, that we might have good reasons for these suspicions? Many people feel they've been let down in recent years: whether it's reasons for going to war in Iraq, phone-hacking, MP expenses, Baby P, Stafford Hospital, Yew-tree, or Hillsborough. Sometimes it's conspiracy, sometimes cock-up. One of us will always remember the Professor of Economics at L.S.E., Luis Garicano, answering the Queen's simple but devastating question as to why no-one had noticed the credit crunch coming: 'At every stage someone was relying on someone else and everyone thought they were doing the right thing.'

So faced with these authorities that we perceive to be disordering our lives and disappointing us time and again, we all need to protect ourselves and we do that by turning to ourselves. We become our own authorities, gatekeepers and filters for what is true and false, right and wrong. We can even shape our spiritual beliefs to fit our own wants and desires.

That's the problem. When someone comes along and tells you that they trust and even live by the contents of a book written a long time ago by dead men – a book that in public consciousness has a 'history' but recently not a glowing one, a book the contents of which might make demands on you, might even say things that you don't want to hear about yourself – then, pardon me, you're going to be very sceptical and wary.

How do you respond to all this?

First, we think you need to try and level up the playing field by getting people to see that your normal day to day living depends upon you trusting authorities all the time. Yes they may let you down but you would not have a society or any kind of order if there were not authority structures in place. We don't deny that principled anarchists exist but we don't see them around that much and we're not sure how consistent they can be (they're principled for a start). Even in popular consciousness we may berate some experts, institutions and authorities, but we love others, don't we? Anyone heard of Simon Cowell?

Moreover, when it comes to things like beliefs and values we all have commitments to things[2] which rest on prior commitments and so on. Although we don't often do it, when we take some time to trace these all

---

2   We think using the word commitment is a more acceptable word than the word 'faith.'

back, we all come to ultimate commitments, be it God, gods, Allah, Brahman, our senses, reason, experience. When we work back to these ultimate commitments, we can't really say these are true because of something or someone behind the commitments which show them to be true, because that would make that some thing or some one more ultimate! For instance, an atheist who defends human rights and is asked why human beings have rights may well reply, 'They just do!' There is no higher value for that atheist that justifies or grounds what she believes. Therefore these ultimate kinds of beliefs are really validated by themselves. We all can tell when we have reached someone's ultimate values by the way he says something along the lines of, 'it just is'.

Now there's lots more we could say here but the point we're making in this book is that a personal God who might choose to reveal himself is in the same 'ultimate' category as all the other ultimates: reason, sense, experience, and so on. While we don't want you to spend a lot of time navel gazing with your friends and doing pop philosophy, we think that getting them to think a bit is quite helpful. For one, it starts to get them questioning the authorities they just assume and never question, and second, it also questions their own questioning of those authorities they have dismissed out of hand. When it comes to ultimate authorities, we're all in the same boat—let's not pretend that at one level, our trust in a God who speaks in the Bible is any different.

We're saying 'at one level' because, on another level, if we understand what the Bible really is then not only should we be given the same trust, certainty and plausibility as other authorities, but we actually have a case to say that we have more trust, certainty and plausibility than these other authorities!

2. We've all got trust issues

Let's talk about issues of trust and certainty. As we've already said, we think that many people today have a self-defence mechanism whereby their authority lies within themselves. So, when we come to things like God and the Bible, people can be very protective and opinionated. They can come across as very certain that 'god is like this,' 'God doesn't exist' or that 'the Bible is just ... (whatever)'. Even people's doubts can be dogmatic: 'We can't be sure about anything ... but I know you are wrong!'

How can you start to melt this hardness?

Our view is that you need to try and point out that human beings are not great when it comes to being their own authority. Let's go back to the radio phone-in example. Although we noted the freedom we have to air our views in public, it doesn't mean that they are any good! One of us often has BBC Radio 5 Live on in his house (because he loves the sport), but even he reaches for the off button when, during a phone-in, a certain type of caller comes on who not only speaks nonsense, but does so in a most dogmatic way, thinking they are the most sensible person in the world. He can't take the cringe factor at this point.

The evangelist Randy Newman has a great illustration he uses to try to pop the arrogance of those who just 'know' that God could not exist. He draws a circle and calls it 'All knowledge'—all that there is to know. He then asks someone to shade in all the knowledge that person currently has. Most people just put a dot in the middle of the circle. Colouring in the rest of the circle he then asks if it's possible that there might be some knowledge in this coloured section that could be evidence of God's existence.[3] Simple but effective. You see people can talk a good game about knowledge but we're limited by our own humanness. We are not God.

Let's put it another way and bring in the Bible. We are going to rehearse something, a little thought experiment. If we step back a bit and ask ourselves a question: how we can get to the place where there is 100 per cent trust anything? We can be 100 per cent sure something's true? To be absolutely 100 per cent sure, we would need to know everything all at the same time. There could not be one stone unturned in the universe, because it might be that under that stone would be evidence to show we'd been wrong all along.

Even something of which we're pretty certain, we can doubt if we want to. Is Antananarivo capital of Madagascar? Someone who claimed so might be lying: he might have faked Google Maps, changed the signs if you go there, drugged you with mind-altering drugs. How would you know to trust anything?

I can present lots of evidence for the Bible, but you can say, 'Maybe those facts are wrong. Maybe you're making all this up. Maybe the documents are fakes. SO I'm not going to trust the Bible and believe in the God of the Bible.'

This is okay, but if you're going to go down the route of, 'You can't 100 per cent prove the Bible to me,

---

3   Randy Newman, *Questioning Evangelism* (Grand Rapids: Kregel, 2004), p. 129.

because there may be other evidence that shows it isn't to be trusted,' then there are some entailments. If we go down that route, then just as you say to me, 'You can't be 100 per cent certain the Bible is to be trusted,' I can say back, 'You can't be 100 per cent certain we shouldn't trust the Bible.' 'Why don't you believe the Bible?' I can ask. And you might say, 'Because I saw a programme that said it was full of errors?' 'Okay', I can say back, 'but are you 100 per cent certain that programme or that book is right? Maybe the "facts" you think disprove the Bible aren't in fact true: maybe there's some evidence against them.' 'Well,' you say, 'I don't think it's trustworthy because it's full of stuff that's just obviously not true. Jesus walking on water, coming back to life, feeding five thousand people with a few loaves.'

But is it really so obvious it's not true? One third of the world are Christians, and believe those things did happen. There are Oxford scientists who believe it. You could hardly say, 'No intelligent person believes it's true.' What makes you so sure those things couldn't happen? It sounds as if you've just plucked that from your prior assumption that God doesn't exist, the very question we're debating anyway!'

The 'I can't be 100 per cent certain, so I'm not going to trust it' argument, you see, would work just as well the other way round: 'I can't be 100 per cent certain the Bible isn't true, so I'll trust it.' Or for that matter: 'I can't be 100 per cent certain atheism is true, so I'll believe in God.'

Unless you know everything, you can never be 100 per cent certain, obviously. That's fair enough. Of course it'd be totally unfair, then, to just apply this to the Bible.

If we're going to be consistent, and we believe this 'You can't be 100 per cent sure about anything' rule, we ought to say, 'I don't fully believe anything, because you can't know for sure.' This is where, if we try to be consistent, we'll end up in madness.

Without wanting to be a clever clogs, if you think about it, we can't even be 100 per cent sure that we can't be 100 per cent sure! Maybe I'm wrong and we can be sure. There's no certainty, remember.

What am I trying to demonstrate here? Is it that being in the same boat means we are all mad and can't trust anything ever? Well no, because I think there is a way out, and one which starts to break down the implausibility of the Bible, and the plausibility of other authorities.

3. 'The Pinocchio problem'

John Frame is a theologian and philosopher. In his book, *Apologetics to the Glory of God*, he conducts another little thought experiment which isn't so much a knockdown proof, but might be delivered as a plausibility punch. He notes that we live in a world of personal beings and impersonal structures and the great question for human beings is: which is more fundamental? Which came first: the personal or the impersonal? Do we ultimately think the personal is explained by the impersonal, or take the opposite view?

Frame goes through the consequences of attempting to show what an impersonal first universe means for our humanity (it's doesn't look good and it doesn't make sense), and then what a personal first universe looks like (makes much more sense). His point is not only to show the unique claims that the God of the Bible is a personal absolute and absolute personality, thus dealing with our desire for both the personal and for absolutes, but also the bias within our cultural context towards the impersonal first, be it fate, the Big Bang, and similar.

As he says, to go the impersonal route first is pretty counter-intuitive and implausible. 'In a factory, human workers produce a tractor (designed and planned by people); a farmer uses that tractor to plough his field. But we have never seen a ploughed field produce a farmer, or a tractor produce a work force.'[4] The only plausible explanation for the idea of the primacy of the impersonal is that the Bible's account of fallen humanity is correct; we suppress the truth no matter how irrational it is to do that.

Let's put it another way. If we were to suppose that the Bible is true, then human beings are made in the image of God, because that's what the Good Book says. God has created humans with brains, and rational thinking abilities. There is a real *you* thinking, a real *you* feeling, a real *you* doing things like reading this chapter.

If the Bible isn't true, and there is no God as the Bible describes, then we can't be made in God's image (because he either does not exist or is very different from the one described). As many suggest – sometimes very loudly – we are just impersonal matter. In that case, Francis Crick would be right: '"You", your joys, and your sorrows, your memories and your ambitions, your sense of personal identity and free will, are in fact no more than the behaviour of a vast assembly of nerve cells and their associated molecules.'[5]

---

4   John Frame, *Apologetics to the Glory of God* (Phillipsburg: P&R, 1994), p. 39.

5   Francis H.C. Crick, *The Astonishing Hypothesis* (New York: Simon and Schuster), 1995, p. 3.

Therefore your emotions as you read this chapter aren't really you. They are just a blind outcome of a huge physical process. Your radio phone-in career: your thoughts, agreeing or disagreeing, your arguments, your questions would all just be the result of reactions set in motion millions of years ago in the Big Bang.

You are built out of chemical DNA which, as we know, are the Lego blocks of life. But like a Lego girl or boy, you are not 'real' or 'alive' or 'personal'. It doesn't matter how many blocks you have, you never become a 'real person'—a bit like Pinocchio.

John Polkinghorne, an Oxford Physicist and Christian, has responded to this, saying that to hold this view is 'ultimately suicidal':

> If Crick's thesis is true we could never know … it … destroys rationality. Thought is replaced by electro-chemical neural events. Two such events cannot confront each other in rational discourse. They are neither right nor wrong. They simply happen … The world of rational discourse dissolves into the absurd chatter of firing synapses. Quite frankly, that cannot be right and none of us believe it to be so.[6]

If there is no God, then all that exists is time and chance acting on matter. As someone put it, the difference between your thoughts and mine correspond to the difference between shaking up a bottle of Diet Coke and a bottle of Dr Pepper. You simply fizz atheistically and I fizz theistically. This means that you do not hold to atheism because it is true, but rather because of a series of chemical reactions. On this account, atheism seems

---

6   John Polkinghorne, *One World,* (London: SPCK), p. 92.

to have problems with (okay, destroys) rationality and morality.

Why call it the Pinocchio problem?

Atheists tend to live as if we're real boys, but also teach that we're just made out of wood. How does that work? At which point did the fairy sweep through the window to bring us to life?

Of course we know that Polkinghorne is right: we are 'real' people with 'real' thoughts capable of rational thought and conversation. But the only way for that to be possible is if we are made as Bible tells us. Personal and real.

So coming back to the Bible, we might trust it, because it's accurate historically. But we also trust it because in it God tells us about himself, and so tells us something about us. Without it we are left in chaos, not knowing anything, and believing ourselves to be impersonal Lego men robots, Pinocchios. In the Bible, God calls us back to obedience, sanity and life.

4. It makes sense, if you ask me

Taking all this one step further, the only point we want to make here is this. If (and, of course, it's a big 'if') we entertain the possibility that there was a personal God – who is the author and creator of all the impersonal and personal stuff in the universe – isn't it conceivable, indeed probable, that this personal God might want to communicate to personal beings? Might he want to do that in a clear and authoritative way? Might such a personal disclosure be verbal, because the information God wants to tell us about – no, better, the person God wants to tell us about and meet (that's the Lord Jesus, by the way) – can't simply be hinted at through a wafty smell, vague impression or a religious sensation? Might this revelation need the specific medium of words, being about historical people, places and events, and including crucially what all these things meant? Might it be sensible that this spoken disclosure would be written down, so it could be preserved, referred to, passed on from generation to generation, from culture to culture? When we break it all down like this, is it all that so far-fetched and ludicrous? Should this way of God communicating be dismissed so readily?

Doesn't this eminently sensible and intuitive way of communicating, in fact, show us our way out of the certainty question? Let's assume the Bible is true, and there is an all-knowing, personal God who cares for us and loves us: and that this God speaks to us. (Remember, we're just supposing for the minute.) Suppose also that this God loved us and was a good God; he'd been prepared, in fact, to sacrifice his own son for us, in order that we could have eternal life. We'd have good grounds for being certain: because we do know someone who knows everything, all at once (because he's God), and he is willing to speak to us and is good and trustworthy. And suppose he tells me the Bible is true. Then I'd trust it, because he knows and he wouldn't lie.

Of course, that's exactly what the Bible does contain—which is ultimately why Christians trust it. I trust because God tells me to.

If I don't believe him, and try to pretend that I live in a universe without an all-knowing God to tell me what's true and what isn't, I'm back stuck in not knowing anything at all, lacking certainty on absolutely every single thing. Or else taking blind faith leaps in the dark. Or pretending I'm God.

Conclusion

Now we might have got carried away a bit here, but do you see our point? We started by saying that when it comes to the Bible, people might be sceptical, cynical and embarrassed that such a topic has come up. However, with a little bit of thought and reflection, we think we can demonstrate that the idea of the Bible is not so crazy after all, but actually makes a great deal of sense. In fact, it makes far more sense than the popular alternative on offer.

Questions

In this chapter we have been talking a lot about putting our trust in a particular authority. In recent years in Europe this has been pretty difficult, as we have found that the leaders we have put our trust in actually have feet of clay. Take this comment from Antonio Barroso:

> In Spain, a recent survey showed that trust and political parties is at 9 per cent, an all-time low. Some 27 per cent of Spaniards have faith in the trade unions, the local councils, and the Supreme Court; 23 per cent expressed confidence in the current government; and just 16 per cent trust the Parliament. In Italy, only 7 per cent trust political parties. The numbers do not look much better in other southern European countries.[7]

---

7   Antonio Barroso, 'Euro Zone: Can Euro-economics Survive Euro-politics?' in I. Bremmer and D. Rediker (Eds), *What's Next: Essays On Geopolitics That Matter* (London: Penguin, 2012), location 202.

And maybe that distrust in institutions goes further than southern Europe.

1. It's easy to mistake someone who is plausible for someone who's trustworthy—an authority in that sense. Please read Isaiah 36:1–37:38 and think through:

    *   Why is the field commander (the Rabshakeh, NRSV, KJV) so plausible?

    *   What kind of trust is he asking for?

    *   Is he worth that kind of trust?

2. What kind of authorities other than the Bible do you trust, and why?

3. What kind of authorities do you see friends and family who are not Christian trusting, and why are they doing so?

3

Reassuringly Unfashionable

One of the biggest challenges to taking the Bible seriously has to do with the perceived cultural offensiveness and irrelevance of the Bible to the enlightened twenty-first century mind. We all know the various hot-spots: sexuality, gender, genocide, slavery, science, judgment, hell, and so on. How do we deal with this perception?

First, we need to ask people, gently and respectfully, to tell us in more detail what specific problems they are talking about, and where they have come from. Then we just listen and see what happens. In our experience, many of these problems are not particularly well formed; in reality, there might be some simple factual things that we can clear up straightaway. Partly this might mean going back to the old issues of authority again. There is a real difference between 'I've got this real problem with issue x in the Bible. I've read it, re-read it, read around it, seen what the alternatives are ...', and 'I saw this documentary on Channel 5 that said ...' (or it might be, 'When we did

R.E. as school, the teacher said ...' or even 'My mate said ...') If a person has problems without ever having opened the Bible itself, isn't this a great opportunity for us to get it open with our friend together, even if we have to go away first and do a little preparation beforehand? Remember that people's doubts about the Bible, which we might think are so strong, are actually beliefs (albeit wrong) about the Bible which they have probably not thought about much and so have taken on faith, which is probably pretty fuzzy-sighted.

Second, we need to get people thinking a little bit about culture and our place in history. Here's an illustration that's been useful in trying to chip away at this negative perception and turn it into a positive. One reason to pick up the Bible and have a look is that it is 'reassuringly unfashionable':

> In the late 80s, the infamous 'Tots' nightclub in South-end-on-Sea had a fancy dress competition every year on Boxing Day. I was desperate to win and so raided my dad's wardrobe for a suitable costume.

> Now my dad was from Guyana in South America and had come over to the U.K. in the late 60s, married my mum and had yours truly. At that time they were a striking couple. My dad was a handsome chap and his clothes and hair in the 70s made him look very similar to Shaft (google it!), complete with Afro and amazing sideburns.

> So just think of the sartorial treasures I uncovered for the fancy dress party – various patterned silk shirts, cravats, medallions (yes, medallions!), bell bottom suede brown flares, etc. Everyone, including me, thought

I looked absolutely ridiculous, outrageous, offensive. I was a walking fashion crime against humanity. I won £10. (Worth a bit back then).

Here's the thing: I know that in the next year or so, my eldest son is going to come to me and say, 'Dad, I've got this fancy dress party coming up, can I have a look in your wardrobe for some clothes crimes, please?'

You see, we still tend to think that our particular stage in the history of humanity is the most enlightened and liberative, that we have a perspective not bound by cultural blind-spots and prejudices. Basically we think that we are 'it'. But we know that in the not-too-distant future, people will look back and think we were so outdated. We do it now. One of us confesses:

I celebrated my twenty-year wedding anniversary a few months ago. Looking through our wedding day photos, at one point I just turned to my wife and said a little crossly, 'Were you playing a practical joke on me in 1994? Why on earth did you allow me to wear those glasses which covered my whole face' – three years before Harry Potter! – 'and that wavy haircut?' But of course, I thought back then I was making the ultimate attempt to look good, and just so she doesn't get out of it, I must say that I think my wife thought I looked good too!

The bottom line is this: are we going to ditch the Bible and its amazing good news for humanity with its eternal implications, just because there is a cultural issue we have now that we know may not be an issue in seventy-five years' time?

We can say a bit more on this. In his little book *Persuasions*, which is an apologetic *Pilgrim's Progress*, Doug

Wilson deals with this issue of the Bible and culture, as the main character, Evangelist, encounters the Rev. Daniel Howe, who questions that the Bible is God's Word. Daniel says to Evangelist:

'It sounds very pious to speak of "God's Word", but you neglect the work of very serious biblical scholars. Modern scholarship indicates that those who wrote the Bible were products of their culture. They wrote as fallible men.'

'You seem to indicate that you think it is not good to be a product of your culture.'

'Why, certainly. If someone writes within the framework of a particular culture, they cannot see it with objectivity.'

'And do modern scholars write from within a culture or not?'

Daniel stopped. 'What do you mean?'

'You don't trust the apostle Paul because he wrote within the first century. Why don't you mistrust modern scholars for the same reason? They write within the twentieth.'

'But modern scholars have good reasons for saying the things they do. They are able to reason objectively.'

'So then, you believe it is possible for a writer to transcend the culture he grew up in?'

'Well, yes.'

'I'm glad to hear you say that. That is what the biblical writers did.'

Daniel appeared to be at a loss for words.

> Evangelist continued. 'We know that the biblical writers were willing to challenge their culture with the Word of God, whenever they saw that such a rebuke was needed. They prophesied and spoke against their contemporaries time and again – far more than modern scholars do. If anyone in history was free of contemporary prejudices they were.'[1]

Because the Bible is what it says it is, not simply a product of culture but a word from another world, although we are earth bound and culture bound, the Bible isn't. We don't sit in judgment over it; it sits in judgment over us.

Finally, we can turn a perceived negative into a positive. In one of his best-ever illustrations Tim Keller asks whether we really want a god who functions as a robot (like the wives do in the film, *The Stepford Wives*), who does everything we say and do, and agrees with everything we say and do. Sure, it might be fun for a while, but this isn't really the stuff of intimate personal relationships which are real ones:

> Now what happens if you eliminate anything from the Bible that offends your sensibility and crosses your will? If you pick and choose what you want to believe and reject the rest, how will you ever have God who can contradict you? You won't! You'll have a Stepford God. A God, essentially, of your own making, and not a God with whom you can have a relationship and genuine interaction. Only if your God can say things that can outrage you and make you struggle (as in a real friend-

---

1   Doug Wilson, *Persuasions* (Moscow, ID: Canon Press, 1989), p. 38.

ship or marriage) will you know that you have got hold of a real God and not a figment of your imagination. So an authoritative Bible is not the enemy of a personal relationship with God. It is a precondition for it.[2]

Questions

Most of us have to cope with people who disagree with us at times and who tell us we've done something unethical and wrong.

- Does it shock you when others disagree with you like this?

- How do you, and how should you, handle it?

- Does it surprise you when God disagrees with you?

- When were you last aware of God disagreeing with you over a course of action?

- How do you, and how should you, handle it when God disagrees with you?

---

2   Tim Keller, *The Reason for God* (London: Hodder, 2008), p. 114.

4

A Perfect Mess

Dan was once talking to a friend of his whose life was unravelling before her eyes. At one point in the conversation she basically said, 'Dan, I love you, but you just don't understand. You can't understand. Your life seems so neat and simple, your faith seems so neat and simple, but real life's complicated, and my life's a mess.'

Now of course Dan wanted to disabuse her of his own personal 'neat and simple' life and faith, but behind his friend's statement was a view that when it came down to it, the Christian faith is not really up to the twists, turns, bumps and bruises of twenty-first century existence. Life is so often fast, fluid, complex, multi-layered, and so often dysfunctional. The Bible is often implicated as a culprit in this charge of simplicity, which is basically one of irrelevance. How can an old book written so long ago understand me and help me in my twenty-first century existence?

What can we say and do about this?

First, we need to make sure that the accusation that the Bible is 'too simple' is not down to someone's 'too simplistic' understanding of what the Bible is. If one sees the Bible as basically a book of blessed thoughts and wise sayings which you pull off the shelf in times of trouble and, fortune cookie-like, apply it to your life, then this charge of 'simple' might stick. We need to get people to think of the Bible more as an incredible story about life, the universe and everything, in which we all show up as characters. For the Christian, the Bible is like a pair of glasses which enables us to get a clear picture of what the world is like. For the authors of this book, it's the first thing that goes on in the morning and last thing that comes off at night.

Second, throughout the ages Christians have recognised in the Bible both a unity and a diversity. The Bible's unity does not mean a boring uniformity of structure and style. The diversity within Scripture does not entail internal contradictions and tensions that would compromise the unity of Scripture, thus rendering Scripture insufficient to be the ultimate authority for Christian faith. Rather, it enhances the richness and depth of the unity of revealed truth. The sixteenth-century theologian Martin Chemnitz put it nicely when he concluded that the gospels exhibited 'a very concordant dissonance'.

When you think about it, there might be method in this messiness. We are not like God in that we don't have an infinite perspective on things. We don't see everything from every angle. We are limited. So it might make sense for God to get us to experience truth from lots of different viewpoints and perspectives.

Okay, but what's the apologetic point of all this? Well, while we must always ultimately affirm peace and harmony between the different parts of the canon of the Bible, we still talk about the messiness of the Bible. What's more, we need to actually big-up this messiness. Randy Newman, in his book *Questioning Evangelism*, includes 'messiness' as a positive factor in getting people to have a look at the Bible. Yes, some might be confused by the Bible's 'hodgepodge construction ...'

> But then again, couldn't these very qualities give credence to the Bible's claims of inspiration and sacredness? Maybe the Bible's messiness corresponds to our messiness, making it the perfect revelation to get us out of our mess. Perhaps its use of various genres corresponds to our complex nature – the intellectual, emotional, volitional, social and physical components of our personhood. Maybe God inspired the Bible to suit our total being.

And as one observer aptly put it:

> If God wants [the Bible] to be a book that interests and challenges people around the globe for their whole lives, that guides us into life's deep mysteries, that trains us to see the world from diverse points of view and in so doing, stretches us to not be so limited by our own inherited point of view, then of course it can't be like a phone book, a government code, or a high school biology text book – easy reference, fully indexed, conveniently formatted for quick easy use. Nor can it be a one-read book, after which we say 'The Bible? Oh, yes, I read that years ago,' implying that we'll never need to look at it or think about it again. If God wants the book to be an authentic medium of spiritual enlightenment and instruction, then how can it be a book that we feel we can fully grasp, have control over, take

pride in our knowledge of, feel competent in regards to? Mustn't it be an untamed book that humbles us, that entices us higher up and deeper in, that renders us children rather than experts, that will sooner master us than we will master it?[1]

While Dan might be perceived as being one-dimensional – neat, and simple and 'sorted' (and as his wife and kids will happily tell you, he's not!) – the Bible is as varied and deep as is humanity—and that makes it so wonderful and glorious and, yes, so incredibly credible.

In an excellent online article by Steve Hays, entitled, *Why I Believe*, he has a section on why he believes the Bible.[2] Two of his factors are relevant here to our messiness point. First is the Bible's psychological realism, which actually points to its historical reality:

The Bible contains a wide variety of psychological portraits—some are thumbnail sketches, others more 3D ... To my mind, and to countless readers before me, their characterisation always rings true. They are unmistakable and unforgettable. Even if a novelistic genius could pull this off, the Bible wasn't penned by a novelist, but by several dozen writers of varied experience. So the only plausible explanation is that we are face-to-face with a record of real people—which is, of course, inseparable from a real life setting.

Second is the Bible's diagnostic discernment:

---

1   Randy Newman, *Questioning Evangelism*, p. 131. The second quotation is from Brian McLaren, *Finding Faith* (Grand Rapids: Zondervan, 1999), p. 233.

2   Steve Hays, *Why I Believe* (accessed 2 October 2014): http://reformed-perspectives.org/article.asp/link/http:%5E%5Ereformedperspectives. org%5Earticles%5Ejoh_frame%5EFrame.Apologetics2004.WhyIBelieve2. Hays.html/at/Why%20I%20Believe%202

The Bible offers a diagnosis of the human condition. On the one hand, it describes the psychology of the believer. On the other hand, it describes the psychology of the unbeliever. And in both cases, its diagnosis is uncannily acute, accurate and prescient. On the one hand, every believer can find himself in the lives of the Old and New Testament saints. On the other hand, unbelievers, past and present, act and react, as if typecast, in exactly the way that Scripture predicts—according to the evasive animosity of John 3:19-21 or the suppress-and-supplant strategy of Romans 1. In this same connection it is striking that Scripture presents the opposing as well as the supporting side. It candidly records the objections of the unbeliever.

What a perfect mess to get ourselves into; what a perfect mess to sort out our own messiness.

Questions

1. We've said that the Bible diagnoses the human condition – it describes us, maybe not by name but by characteristics. Which parts of the Bible's descriptions of human beings do you think most clearly describe you?

2. Think again of that friend or relative who is not a Christian. What parts of the Bible (in terms of genre, style, content and so forth) might resonate most with them and their character? What parts might jar with them most? How might this reflection affect your witness to them?

5

The Greatest Gift this World Affords

– or 'What's the Bible ever done for us?'

Introduction

The American comedian Jerry Seinfeld has a great routine where he muses on numerous studies which have shown that people's number one fear is public speaking. Death is number two. He goes on, 'This means to the average person, if you go to a funeral, you're better off in the casket than doing the eulogy.'

This fear was given dramatic significance in the critically acclaimed film, *The King's Speech*. Portraying both personal story and national crisis, the film focuses on the remarkable relationship between Albert, Duke of York, who would become King George VI, and his speech therapist, the unorthodox and 'colonial commoner' Lionel Logue. The noble is suffering from a debilitating stammer and is seen in every way to be 'unfit' for the role of monarch.

If you've seen the film, you'll know that the film opens with a nightmarish scene as Albert prepares to give a speech before the Empire Exhibition at Wembley Stadium in 1925. The excruciating stammer with which he has been afflicted noticeably unsettles and embarrasses those present in the stadium. The film closes with Albert's three-page radio speech given upon the declaration of war with Germany in 1939. While by no means a piece of accomplished oratory, it is a speech which displays enough drama and authority to bring some comfort and reassurance to the millions of British citizens huddled around their wirelesses on the eve of war.

As we've pointed out in previous chapters, another King's speech – the King's speech which is the Bible – appears to have suffered a reversal of fortune similar to that of dear old 'Bertie' with regards to its standing in British public and cultural life. It's bad enough that people have all kinds of problems with the Bible in terms of its rationality, morality and even relevance. Frankly, it's viewed a bit like that eccentric wider family member: the Bible is a bit of an embarrassment. What's worse is that the Bible is simply not on people's radar. This is worse than irrelevance because at least if you think the Bible is irrelevant, you're still talking about the Bible. No, this is about people never entertaining any thoughts about the Bible. You don't believe us? Well we refer you back to the little section on illiteracy in Chapter 1.

How do we deal with this?

As we have shown in Chapter 1, we all simply need to get down to the slow and often painstaking task of re-education. Here we are not just talking about re-educating people as to what the Bible says it is, its story and characters and its message about Jesus (crucial as that is). We are saying in this book more about a basic educational lesson that demonstrates the influence that the Bible has had in history and, more specifically, in our Western history. One big reason the Bible is ignored is because people are ignorant of its impact. In a subtle way, we need to get the Bible back into our culture's consciousness. We need to help people understand where they have come from, and that some of the ideas and ideals they cherish most are there because of the impact of the Bible. There are severe cases of historical myopia and amnesia which need remedying. Put bluntly, we need to big-up the Bible more! All this would help in our pursuit of plausibility.

Now the two of us sometimes think that we Christians are quite reticent about doing this educating, maybe even a little scared. Perhaps we all think that by talking about the cultural impact of the Bible in our society we might come across as arrogant, triumphalistic and even imperialistic, linking the Bible to tricky issues of national identity, multiculturalism and racism. But we can talk about the Bible's impact without having strains of 'Land of Hope and Glory' in the background, or, worse still, having to vote for the B.N.P.

Perhaps we all think that by talking about the past like this we are simply wallowing in nostalgia and senti-mentality, guilty of indulging in what we both expressly said we should not do in Chapter 1, when we quoted from Ecclesiastes 7:10: 'Do not say, "Why were the old days better than these?"' But by talking about the Bible's impact, are we simply talking about the past? Yes, the Bible's influence has been massively marginalised in the last few hundred years. However, while the account may be dwindling fast, we both would argue that there is still 'biblical cultural capital' that as a culture we secretly but unknowingly continue to draw from and that needs to be named and not shamed, but rather honoured.

So if we've got over these two obstacles, I'm sure we'll all now be bursting for appropriate times to speak about the impact of the Bible in our cultural life—or will we? We probably need to admit that as Christians we don't actually know this history as well as we should. We're not immune from versions of our history where talk of the Bible's impact has been airbrushed out and graffitied over. We probably need to do a bit of revision as well. What's good (and what stops this becoming a long chapter), is that there is some excellent and very readable stuff on the impact of the Bible.[1] What's really good is that in doing this revision, we both hope you'll be encouraged to see the amazing transformative power of the Bible and its message, not just in changing individual lives, but to change communities and transform cultures. Such encouragement should then issue in praise and glory for the God who brings about such change.

Here are some edited highlights to get us going.

We begin by staying with the theme of royalty, indeed the very same Windsor family. Whether one is a royalist or not, or even whether one takes any of the 'pomp and circumstance' of monarchy as being at all relevant to British life and culture, surely we can at least note the words in the Coronation ceremony of Queen Elizabeth II in June 1953. It was with the following words from the

---

1   One of the best is by the Indian scholar, Vishal Mangalwadi, *The Book That Made Your World: How the Bible created the Soul of Western Civilisation,* Thomas Nelson, 2011.

Archbishop of Canterbury that Her Majesty received a copy of the Bible:

> Our gracious Queen: to keep your Majesty ever mind-ful of the Law and the Gospel of God as the Rule for the whole life and government of Christian Princes, we present you with this Book, the most valuable thing that this world affords. Here is Wisdom; This is the royal Law; These are the lively Oracles of God.

While there are those in all sectors of a monarchy who wish it were not so, one cannot deny the relevance, role, and yes, even rule, that the Bible has explicitly played in the shaping of British life and culture. As the author P.D. James summarises concerning the 'Authorized Version': 'No book has had a more profound and lasting influence on religious life, the history and the culture, the institutions and the language of the English-speaking peoples throughout the world than has the King James Bible.'[2]

It is likely that within two hundred years of Jesus's birth Britannia had heard the Christian message, but it was not until A.D. 511 and the preaching of Patrick, Columba, Aiden, and Augustine that Christian numbers and influence increased. The earliest document written in English is the law code of Ethelbert, which was strongly influenced by biblical ideals and law. The common law system developed during the twelfth and thirteen centuries was largely shaped by Christian values. Many aspects of the British justice system that its citizens cherish – retributive justice, legal representation,

---

2   Cited in Susan Elkin, 'Restoring Holy Order', *The Independent* (October 17, 2010), http://www.independent.co.uk/arts-entertainment/books/features/restoring-holy-order-is-the-king-james-bible-the-only-version-we-should-celebrate-2105869.html.

the taking of oaths, judicial investigation, and rules for evidence – all owe a debt to a huge Christian influence based on the biblical revelation.

In a similar vein, inscribed in Latin over the door of the physics laboratory in Cambridge is neither 'Physics is fun' nor 'Leave your faith before entering' but Psalm 111:2: 'Great are the works of the Lord, studied by all those who delight in them,'[3] a verse chosen by the scientist and formulator of electromagnetic theory, James Clerk Maxwell. The foundation of the Royal Society in the seventeenth century stated that it wished to demonstrate 'the power and wisdom, the goodness of the Creator as it is displayed in the admirable order, and workmanship of the Creatures'. We see this in the writings of William Harvey, Isaac Newton, Robert Boyle and John Ray.

Then there are, of course, the areas of social reform and transformation, human rights, dignity and tolerance. We know it's the stuff of Hollywood, because it's become Hollywood. For forty-six years between 1787 and 1833 William Wilberforce fought tirelessly for the abolition of the African Slave Trade. The Bill was defeated eleven times before, at 4.00 a.m. on 23 February 1807, the Bill succeeded: At one point 'the House rose almost to a man and turned towards Wilberforce in a burst of Parliamentary cheers. Suddenly above the roar of "hear, hear" and quite out of order, three hurrahs echoed and echoed while he sat, head bowed, tears streaming down his face.' As one eminent historian has said: 'from any historical perspective, this was a stupendous transformation'.

---

3   'Magna opera Domini exquisita in omnes voluntates ejus.'

What motivated Wilberforce? What made Wilberforce tick? Was he just a jolly nice chap? Was it about political and economic gain? Was it his general belief in human rights and human dignity? Even given the mixed motivations in all our actions, it seems clear that Wilberforce's biblical faith was a major factor. What people might not know is that alongside his campaigning, Wilberforce wrote a tract in 1797 with the snappy title: *A Practical View of the prevailing Religious system of professed Christians in the Higher and Middle Classes in this country contrasted with Real Christianity*. We shouldn't mock: it became a google and by 1826 fifteen editions had been printed and it had been translated into numerous languages. In this tract Wilberforce speaks of:

> The fatal habit of considering Christian morals as distinct from Christian doctrines insensibly gained strength. Thus the peculiar doctrines of Christianity went more and more out of sight and as might naturally have been expected, the moral system itself also began to wither and decay, being robbed of that which should have supplied it with life and nutriment. At length, in our own days, these peculiar doctrines have almost altogether vanished from our view.

Even in 1797, Wilberforce recognised something that we need to be constantly emphasising today: you can't have Christian morals without those 'peculiar doctrines' of Christianity, those doctrines that are contained exclusively in God's revealed written words in the Bible. This Bible not only gives us ethical standards and norms which we all need, but a Saviour to rescue us when we break these standards. This is the good news of the gospel: 'of a sinner's acceptance with God.'[4] In

---

4   William Wilberforce, *A Practical View of Preferred Christians* (Cosima, Inc., 2005), p. 47.

the world we all say that we want, the Bible needs to be front and centre. Without it we will continue to wither and decay.

We could both continue and talk about the Bible's influence in medicine, in technological advancement, in economic development, in education, and in literature. But we'll let you read up on these yourselves. Let's not be ashamed of the Bible but recognise its role and impact in our culture.

'What has the Bible ever done for us?' Quite a lot, actually.

Questions

1. What is the rational basis for saying that the world would be a better place if the Bible had never been written?

2. In his book *Why We Should Call Ourselves Christians*, Marcello Pera argues that the concept of political freedom we enjoy in the West comes from our Christian heritage. In fact, he says we continue to depend on our Christian heritage to underpin those freedoms. He writes:

   Without the Christian vision of the human person, our political life is doomed to become the mere exercise of power and our science to divorce itself from moral wisdom; our technology to become indifferent to ethics and material well-being blind to our exploitation of others and our environment.[5]

---

5   Marcello Pera, *Why We Should Call Ourselves Christians* (New York & London: Encounter Books, 2011), chapter 1.

Please think through/discuss these two questions that come from Pera's words:

- Do you agree with him?
- Where could the 'Christian vision of the human person' come from other than the Bible?

6

It's Not About You

It's a real privilege to belong to a Christian community which constantly reminds me, because I need to be constantly reminded, that I am saved by grace through Christ and not by works, that I'm accepted by God so I obey, not I obey so I'm accepted. Grace, Grace, Grace.

Salvation by grace alone is a pretty fundamental communication in describing what the Christian faith is. Given the absolute centrality of this truth, you'd think wouldn't you, that people who reject Christianity today are rejecting the idea of salvation by grace? But how is it that time after time, the non-Christians we speak to think that the central message of Christianity is about being a good person and doing good things? How is it that the popular view of Christianity is not a little wobbly and fuzzy, but the exact opposite of what is actually the case? Both of us have got some ideas on this but they'll have to wait I'm afraid. A little tip for us all though: please don't presume that people know what the good news of Jesus is, or what a Christian is. Presume nothing; explain everything.

Why have we started with this point? Well, when it comes to the Bible, we think there is a similar gross misunderstanding. We've already mentioned it in an earlier chapter. For many people the Bible, if it's anything at all, is a human book with good bits and bad bits. The good bits contain general and universal blessed thoughts and wise sayings applied to their lives. They might know a couple of phrases; they might even have something written down somewhere for inspiration, along with other phrases by Einstein, the Buddha, Confucius, Deepak Chopra, Paul McKenna and Stephen Fry.

For others, the Bible is recognised as a great work of literature which has been important in cultural life and the arts: literature, painting, and music. It can be acknowledged and should be studied for the preservation of culture, and may even say some profound things about the human condition, a bit like Shakespeare, but that's about it really.

For yet others, even some Christians, the Bible functions a little bit like the installation disc for my computer printer. I might have used it once when I got my printer (and then I certainly didn't read the accompanying guide from cover to cover), but now it just sits in my box of old computer cables unless I need to trouble-shoot, and then actually I can go elsewhere to find help.

Is this what the Bible is about, just some personal home-spun wisdom, just a great human work of literature, just a trouble-shooting guide for my life?

Of course not! As we've said already, what we need to get across is that the Bible is that pair of glasses through which we see life, the universe and everything. It's the story of the universe, the greatest story ever told that orientates us in our world, telling us who we are, where we have come from, and where we are going. It should excite us and thrill us. It should get inside our head just like our favourite piece of music that we turn to again and again, finding new things to listen to. Or that favourite film that we lose ourselves in, even though we've watched it a thousand times.

The Bible is the genuine original of which all others are imitators, with its perennial themes of innocence, loss, guilt, redemption. It's reassuringly expansive. Of course it's going to be deep and complex in places because it's served as the foundation for governments as well as providing the most amazing stories for children. As St Jerome famously put it: 'The Scriptures are shallow enough for a babe to come and drink without fear of drowning and deep enough for theologians to swim in without ever reaching the bottom.'

Okay, okay, but bottom line: what's the Bible about? What pulls it all together?

The overwhelming view is that the Bible is about me. It's some kind of rulebook that I obey. We can't do it, so we feel crushed. It's a great work of literature, about us as humans, to be studied. It's that troubleshooting book, when I'm in trouble.

But this is missing the point. We hit the bull's eye when we remember how Luke narrates the apostle Philip's response to the Ethiopian eunuch's request to help him understand a passage in Isaiah: 'Then Philip began with that very passage of Scripture and told him the good news about Jesus' (Acts 8:35).

The Bible is not first about me, about us, about humanity. It's about someone else. The Bible points to, and is explained by, the most amazing figure history has ever witnessed: Jesus Christ. As Steve Hays[1] puts it:

> When we read the Bible, we can identify with almost every character. Some of them are better than us, others worse. Yet we can project ourselves into either persona. But there is one singular and surpassing exception. In Christ we encounter a figure who is at once one with us and yet apart from us, who inspires admiration and defies emulation. He has fellow feeling without loss of firmness, and familiarity without hint of complicity. He can speak at the level of a child, yet with a reserve of subtlety that leaves the keenest listener out of his depth. No other figure, in either fact or fiction, covers such a range and/or strikes such a balance, for in him we witness perfect manhood and perfect Godhood conjoined in one peerless person.

This peerless person is Jesus Christ, the Son of God, who comes to earth from heaven, who teaches with a unique authority, who says that all of the Bible is about him (John 5:39). Jesus, who is both standard and Saviour. Jesus, who releases the tension set up throughout the rest of the Bible (how can people have a relationship with a personal God?). Jesus, who lays down his life, taking the place of rebels who have not trusted but rebelled against God. Jesus, who is risen

---

1   See Chapter 4, footnote 2.

from the dead, who is alive now, who has ushered in a new creation. Jesus, who calls us to follow him.

This is a book about the Bible; it's about having confidence in the Bible. But, I don't have a personal relationship with the Bible, I don't worship the Bible. It is because of the Bible, however, that I have met Jesus Christ my Lord, and I trust what the Bible says about him.

At the end of the day, when all is said and done, we want to talk about the Bible because we want to talk about Jesus. We want to be always heading in a Jesus direction.

Questions
Please read John 5:39-46 and think through/discuss the following questions:

- Does Jesus think it matters if we think that the Bible is not a testimony to him?

- What kind of sense will the Bible make if we think it is not primarily a testimony to Jesus?

PART TWO:

A Word for Us

Where does the Bible fit into the life of a church or a Christian? There is considerable puzzlement about this amongst Christians today. Christians in local churches would largely say that the Bible does have authority. That is right as far it goes, but the issue is not whether it has authority but rather how much authority it has. This question of how much authority the Bible has becomes decisive when we try to work out how what the Bible says fits together with the other sources of knowledge we use. Do some of those other sources of knowledge trump the Bible? Or does the Bible trump them? Perhaps they all have an authority? But which, if any, comes first?

This question matters so much because we human beings need to know what God is like and what he wants for us and for our lives. We rightly feel that we don't want Christianity to be of just academic interest or just a matter of words. We want to know God in our hearts as well as our heads and we want to know his will for us personally.

So, how does an authentic, personal and mature Christian faith treat the Bible?

Key Summary

The short answer is that we should treat the Bible in the same way Jesus does. So, in Mark 7 Jesus teaches that there is a key distinction between two different kinds of words, the word of God and words which are purely human. This distinction is key, because if we get it wrong, it means that our worship is in vain and our hearts are far from God. This consequence follows from who we are and who God is. This distinction carries huge implications for how we read and understand the Bible. Elsewhere Jesus treats the Bible as necessary, trustworthy, coherent and centred on him, and sufficient for its purposes.

The rest of this little book teases this out as we look at a number of things:

- the shape of the puzzle we face in weighing the Bible and other sources of knowledge;

- what underlies Mark 7, and what that means for us as we read the Bible as those seeking to grow in a mature, personal, Christian faith;

- how Jesus uses the Bible in his own life.

7

Says Who?
The Questions of Authority

Introduction

We have already mentioned that we face a question about how the Bible fits in with our other sources of knowledge. After all, Christians come across all kinds of things that count as alternative or additional sources of knowledge. Just imagine a Christian driving to church: she uses her knowledge of how to understand petrol gauges to check she has enough fuel, her recollection of the Highway Code to let a bus pull out in front of her, her experience of driving to keep well clear of the car in front that's weaving across the road, and so on. She uses all kinds of different knowledge and understanding just to get to church. But let's break these different kinds of knowledge down a bit more systematically.

Kinds of knowledge

1. The world outside

Sometimes those other sources of knowledge are what the world outside the churches thinks it has discovered as it pursues its own learning in the humanities and sciences. One example would be findings or proposals about the historical situation in which a part of the Bible was written. Thus some scholars suggest that 1 Corinthians 7 is written against the background of an economic slump and food shortages in Corinth. Others argue that the plausibility of early Christians and their faith needs to be seen against a backdrop of their impressive selfless care for others during the outbreak of plague in the second and third-century Roman Empire. Another example is the proposal drawn (very controversially) from biological sciences that same-sex attraction is genetically determined or at least genetically influenced.

2. The world inside

There again, some of these sources of knowledge that people rely on besides the Bible come not from the world outside but from inside us. Thus some within our churches think the idea of the Trinity is self-contradictory and in consequence should either be dropped altogether or taught only very sparingly. Here the other source of knowledge is our own rational sense of what is or is not possible, whatever the Bible says. Effectively, our ideas of logic, and of what is possible, and how all that applies to a particular question, become that other source of knowledge.

In this example of the Trinity, what we sense as possible or rational can make us not necessarily deny but certainly downplay a particular aspect of biblical teaching. It is important to note this last point: sometimes our alternative source of knowledge may not always lead us to straight denial of something in the Bible but to a downgrading of it in terms of weight and significance, and consequently a turning-down of the volume on it in public discussion and proclamation.

Another example relates not so much to my idea of what is rationally possible, but rather to what I intuitively feel. I may see those intuitive feelings as a source of knowledge for a number of reasons: perhaps I think sin has not rendered human consciences radically unreliable but that rather all humans actually have a largely reliable sense of right and wrong. Thus some argue, wrongly we both think, that John 1:9 means that each human being always has the divine light inside them so that they can tell right from wrong, truth from falsehood.[1] Alternatively I may see the Holy Spirit as so renewing my heart and mind that since becoming a Christian my inner sense of God's truth has been made largely reliable. Some suggest John 16:13 supports this, again wrongly in our view.[2] A variant on this last possibility, of course, is the idea that a local church congregation gathered together in its meeting, or a denomination gathered in its assembly or synod, has collectively a largely, or even infallibly, reliable sense of what is right.

3. A clash of knowledge?

Now what happens when one of these sources of knowledge conflicts with the Bible? This may be an explicit conflict, or it may be implicit, by necessary

---

1   The context of John 1:9 makes it almost impossible for it to refer to an illumination of each human individual. If there was such an illumination, then humanity and the covenant people would not have rejected the true Light in the way that John 1:10-11 makes it clear they did.

2   John 16:13 most naturally construed is a promise to Jesus's apostles that they will by the Spirit understand what he has taught in his incarnation before the Ascension. It is therefore historically specific and not a general promise to Christians of all ages that they will be led into more and more truth.

logical consequence. This moment of conflict is also the moment of truth for showing how we view these sources of knowledge, and how we rank them in comparison with each other. Many Christians are very happy to use external sources of knowledge (I am writing this using a laptop, and the Bible is largely silent on laptops), and many Christians would also want to testify to the work of the Spirit not merely in illuminating us to have faith in Jesus Christ, but also in sensitising our consciences over time to things about which we used to be indifferent. But when, say, my inner sense of what God is like conflicts with what the Bible says about him, I find out not so much that I think the Bible has authority, but rather how much authority it has. I find out what its place is in my hierarchy of sources of knowledge. I find out whether I think it has supreme authority, or whether it can be trumped by something else.

This is not, of course, a problem that only occurs with the Bible. There are many different occasions in all kinds of areas of life when we have to decide how much authority a source of information has. We may overhear a conversation on the bus that mentions that a politician is thinking of resigning, but we do not believe it until it is cited on the web by a reputable daily. I may hear from a close friend that fish oil will make my brain work better through helping my synapses work faster, but, since I have also read in the responsible journal *New Scientist* that this is unsupported by any research other than that generously sponsored by the British Cod-Liver Oil Association, I refuse to subject myself to the rigours of cod-liver oil every morning. In these examples, I have a hierarchy of sources of knowledge. In the cod-liver oil case, those sources clash, and the authority for me of *New Scientist* is shown by the way that I listen to its judgment rather than my friend's, even though I know her and like her, in contrast to the *New Scientist*.

So too with the Bible. We start to see not just that we think it has authority, but how much authority it has when it comes into conflict with what claims to be knowledge from other sources. These conflicts between competing claims for our beliefs reveal which we trust more, and which has more authority for us in that sense.

In particular, some sincere people within today's churches think that with 2,000 years, more knowledge of the world and the chance to reflect on what God has already done and said, we can develop our thinking and teaching beyond what the Bible teaches, or even against what the Bible teaches.

One very important consideration in this line of thought is that we can spot where the Bible is going with some of its ideas, and can take that thinking further along what we might call the Bible's trajectory of travel. By trajectory I mean the path or direction along which something is going. (For instance the trajectory of computer development has been to create more and more memory in later models.) This means that when you have spotted what the trajectory of an idea is, you can predict what the next step of its development is: you can see where it is going. When it comes to the Bible, this idea of trajectory is in a sense simply trying to apply a particular biblical idea or passage as richly as we can. The crunch comes when some go so far along what they see as the Bible's trajectory from some passages that they adopt a position that is at odds with what the Bible explicitly says in other passages. At this point they have ended up with an application of one part of the Bible that contradicts another but explicit part of the Bible.

Thus, a highly topical example of this trajectory kind of argument is the debate about same-sex marriage. The idea of trajectory weighs heavily with many of those within our churches who argue that same-sex marriage is permitted by God. The argument is that one can discern a trajectory within Scripture towards a view of marriage that stresses lifelong fidelity and commitment to one partner, and that if this quality of relationship is present then marriage is permitted irrespective of gender. This, though, stands at odds with the way New Testament passages such as Romans 1:26-28 and 1 Corinthians 6:9 explicitly see same-sex sexual intercourse as sinful, and also with how Genesis 2 deals with male and female as complementary genders, implying that same-sex marriage is not possible as a matter of our creation.

We should point out here for the sake of completeness that obviously some arguing for same-sex marriage want to produce a different interpretation of those passages. Those alternative interpretations do not in any case rest on adequate reasons in our view. But for our present purposes, what matters is that there are those who think these New Testament passages do indeed teach that same-sex marriage is forbidden, but who feel that the overall trajectory of the Bible means that we can now see that these passages are wrong at least in our time.

4. Why does all this matter?

It sounds obvious to say that it matters how much authority Christians give to the Bible. Even so, this is worth spelling out. Christians, of course, are already committed on the question of whether God exists, that is, whether he is there at all. The question of God's existence certainly does matter when sharing the Gospel of Christ with those who do not believe, but amongst ourselves we speak and conduct ourselves on the basis that this question at least is settled. We presume it is true, and do not act as if it is not true or still up for debate.

Instead, for Christians the key theological questions have moved on from whether there is a God to two central issues: first, what he is like; and secondly, what his will is for us. Earlier theologians in the Reformation period (notably John Calvin) thought true Christian theology was all about these two questions. On the first question, when we seek out what he is like, we are searching to understand his characteristics and attributes—what it means for him to be infinite and eternal, and what it means to be three persons, Father, Son and Holy Spirit, in one substance.

This understanding of what God is like is not just a matter of academic interest. It is intimately related to the second question—what is his will for us? Thus, if his will is that we worship him, we need to know something about what he is like in order to worship him as he is, rather than ascribing all kinds of false characteristics to him. We might almost say that the second half of the book of Exodus is about just this question of worship— God sets out how he is to be worshipped, and, as the golden calf incident of Exodus 32 shows, not all worship is acceptable to God. This is reinforced by passages such as Jeremiah 7:31, where God speaks of those who have passed their children through the fire, ostensibly in worship. God denies this was his intention or that it honours him. This warns us that we may offer to God what we might think is acceptable worship but actually is not what he thinks is acceptable. Similarly in Acts 17:22-31, Paul instructs the Athenians not to continue with their current ways of thinking about God and consequently wrongly worshipping him.[3] God's will is central for how we relate to him, especially in worship.

Of course, it could be easy to feel that this talk of God's will is not so much about God's authority, but about authoritarianism. Some teachers in our churches say that God does not want to restrict us, but wants us instead to flourish and enjoy ourselves and fulfil our potential through experiment of all kinds. He aims for us to express our autonomy and in fact simply wants us to enjoy life and thrive. On first hearing, this sounds as though God does not have a will for us. But surprisingly this, too, eventually ends up as a question of God's will. This is because the underlying justification for our claims to be left to thrive as we autonomously see fit comes from what we say God wants. At the end of the day, the argument for such freedoms for us turns precisely on the point that we think that this is a freedom that God wants for us. This means it boils down again to a question of God's will for us. That in turn makes us ask, 'How do we know that is God's will for us?'

This second question, of what God's will is for us, must not be ignored. The first question, of who God is, has a breath-taking and awe-inspiring fascination, while this second question stresses the relational and in fact personal nature of Christian theology. We are not just finding out what God is like to wile away an idle in-

---

3   See verse 29, following Paul's 'deconstruction' of Athenian worship in terms of holy place and holy offering in verses 24-28.

tellectual hour, nor simply to find out what he wants as a matter of generality for humans overall: I want to know and need to know what his will is for me personally in my own individual relationship with him.

Conclusion: The killer question

Thus Christians at the moment, faced with these puzzles, need to know how an authentic, personal and mature faith rightly treats the Bible. Is the Bible more than just one authority amongst other equal authorities; is it in fact supremely authoritative as it addresses the questions of what God is like, and what his will is for us? By supremely authoritative, we are referring to the way that the Bible's verdict on a question about God and his will must be preferred over all other sources of knowledge.

Before we move on, we need to note the scope of the way we have just put this question. The issue is what the Bible reveals about what God is like, and what his will is for our lives, not whether the Bible provides definitive guidance on DNA sequencing, or the economic pressures that faced Alexander the Great and helped to propel him on wars of conquest, fascinating though that might be in its right place.

Questions

Quite often in our culture you hear something like this: 'It doesn't matter what you believe as long as you're sincere' or 'I just worship God in my own little way'. Please read Romans 1:18-23, and look especially at verse 21. Then think through/discuss the following questions:

- How does this passage show us that sincerity is not enough?

- What we need to know in order to 'worship God as God'? Who is best placed to know?

Going deeper #1

Trajectory talk: Where's it all heading?

The idea of 'trajectory' has come to be an important feature in recent discussions, so it is worth spending a little time on 'trajectory', and when it is useful. While 'trajectory' arguments have been much used over the last few years, it is not clear that people always realise what is at stake in how this fits into good handling of the Bible. Three issues are especially relevant here.

First, there is the issue of whether one thinks the Bible is basically coherent and that in God's providence it is not self-contradictory, because God is not self-contradictory. (We will tease out a little later why *who we think God is* must affect *what we think the Bible is*.) If we think that is right, then we will not interpret one part of the Bible to contradict another part—we will seek ways of harmonising different parts of the Bible. This is a perfectly standard approach. Thus Article 20 of the Church of England's *Thirty-nine Articles of Religion* states that one part of the Bible is not to be interpreted in a way that is 'repugnant' or contradictory to another.

Secondly, if we think the Bible is ultimately coherent and fits together, then we will feel able to use one part of the Bible to interpret another. At its simplest this can mean using Mark's Gospel to interpret Matthew's. In a more complex way, we may use the thoughts about wisdom of, say, Job 28 to bring us to a fuller and more rounded understanding of what Paul teaches about the limitations of human wisdom in 1 Corinthians 1 and 2. Naturally we will want to take care as we do this, and make sure we are comparing like with like. Moreover, frequently we will let what is expressed in one passage, or is stated relatively clearly, help us to interpret a passage where an idea may only be implicit at best or simply unclear.

Thirdly, Christians have recognised for centuries that we need to apply the Bible, by which we mean taking what the Bible teaches on specific matters, and seeing how that can rightly and logically apply more widely. Thus Proverbs regularly warns against use of the tongue and how we speak. A ready twenty-first century application would be how we express ourselves on Twitter or other social media: not exactly use of the tongue, but involving the same principles.

Now, we need to draw those three issues together.

Application is something we must do. We want to give the Bible its full range of application. Apart from anything else, we see Jesus doing this in the Sermon on the Mount in Matthew 5–7, where he regularly brings out a principle which the original Law from Mount Sinai expressed. He then applies that principle more widely, for example, going beyond physical actions to the heart in the prohibitions on murder and adultery.

This means that, where a trajectory line of argument is trying to do this task of application, then it is in principle attempting something worthwhile and important. However, it is also possible to do this task of application, or trajectory-creation, badly.

We would be applying the Bible – or a part of it – badly if we were to interpret it in a way that made it contradict other parts of the Bible. Thus, it would be bad application to say that the law 'love your neighbour' meant you could have a sexual affair with your neighbour and be unfaithful to your own spouse—that would be loving your neighbour in a sinful way. This would be true even if you felt very fond of your neighbour and didn't just see him or her as an opportunity for sexual fulfilment. We know that taking the command to love your neighbour like this is a misapplication, because it is an interpretation that applies the command, 'love your neighbour', in such a way that it contradicts the express command 'do not commit adultery'. Instead, the first two issues we have described above – that the Bible is coherent and that we interpret one part of the Bible by other parts of the Bible– mean we can check whether an application or trajectory is a good one or not. We cannot assume that, just because it claims to be an application or trajectory, it is automatically good.

This is why the use of a 'trajectory' argument in the same-sex debate has proved so disturbing. It runs the risk of claiming biblical authority for a position because it is allegedly an application of the Bible, but in fact it does violence to the coherence of the Bible. It does so by producing something which contradicts the express teaching of the Bible in the texts we have already referred to. This means that something which is unexpressed and at best an inferred application, namely that same-sex marriage is permissible, is being preferred to a contrary set of commands which are explicit. This, of course, is quite contrary to the normal – and to be frank, sensible – ways of interpreting the Bible.

What this means in practice is that when we or others make claims about how a biblical passage applies, or what its trajectory is, we must tests those claims: not just as possible inferences from a particular pet passage, but for overall fit and coherence with the rest of the Bible, and especially for lack of contradiction with other express and clear passages.

8

Says Jesus
Treating the Bible as Jesus does

Introduction

We have outlined our key question in terms of how much authority the Bible has. In fact, we can tie it down a little more closely still: 'How much authority should a Christian think the Bible has?' When we stop and think about it, it is not obvious that Christians, atheists and believers in other religions, are going to give anything like the same answer to this authority question. Many atheists are going to think that biblical authority is a non-issue, since their belief that there is no God will dictate answers both to the question of what he is like and what his will is for us. Similarly, a convinced white witch will naturally be coming with strong preconceptions about how much authority the Bible has. But our question is about how much authority a Christian should rightly think the Bible has.

To answer that, we start first with how Christians should generally shape their lives. There is a very basic proposition here. Christians should shape their lives on the model of Jesus. Accordingly, the starting point for how Christians should treat the Bible is simply this: Christians should treat the Bible in the same way that Jesus does.

Christians, after all, take their name from Jesus Christ. Christian faith over the centuries has insisted that Jesus is unique as God's eternal Son and Saviour of the world. We believe something distinctive about Christ: that he lived a life that pleased God in every way and in particular that he is, using traditional terminology, God's unique prophet, priest and king.

It is worth spending a minute, however, thinking through what it would mean if we rejected the idea that we should treat the Bible in the same way that Jesus does. If we did reject this idea, we might mean either that we treated the Bible with more authority than Jesus does, or that we treat it with less authority than he does. As we shall see, it is difficult to treat the Bible as being more authoritative than Jesus does, since Jesus sees it in a very strong way as being God's Word. However, what about the other alternative, namely that we treat the Bible as having less authority than Jesus does?

1. Treating the Bible as having less authority than Jesus thought

If we did treat the Bible as having less authority for us than for Jesus, it almost inevitably suggests that we know more about what God is like and what his will is for us than Jesus does. After all, we would be making a judgment that said we know that the Bible does not in fact express God and his will as well as Jesus thinks it does.

Jesus may think that the Bible is necessary for a perfect human life with God, but we know that it is not. What is more, we should stress that the issue here is not whether someone knows about, say, the existence of America; it is knowing what God is like, and what his will is. It is important to keep the scope of our inquiry in mind here. Even if we did think that Jesus in his human nature did not know as much about how the sun worked as we do in terms of nuclear fusion, it does not follow that he knows less than we do about what God is like, what his will is, and where it is expressed. The question is how much we believe Jesus knows about how to lead a perfect human life before God.

a. The uniqueness of Jesus as a prophet and king

If we did think that we knew better than Jesus what God is like and what his will is – so that we could safely attribute less authority to the Bible than he does – then it would be hard to see how that would be consistent with the unique position of Jesus in two respects: that of prophet and king.

To begin with, Jesus certainly is a prophet and revealer (naturally, in traditional language, he is priest and king as well as prophet). Prophets, of course, in various ways speak for God to his people. They may remind God's people of what he has already said, and call them back to faithfulness. They may explain and interpret something that is happening, as when Jeremiah interprets the invasions that the kingdom of Judah is suffering. They may foretell what God is going to do, as when Jesus' birth in Bethlehem is foretold. Overall, prophets express God's will to his people. They express God's will as revealed in the past, as it is to be understood in the present, and as it will be fulfilled in the future.

Jesus, however, is unique as a prophet, because he is the eternal Son. This uniqueness of the way that Jesus reveals God is brought out in Hebrews 1, where the writer draws a distinction between what Jesus brings in terms of God's speaking in the writer's day and what the earlier prophets brought. The point is that while God did indeed speak in 'many times and in various ways' by the prophets, in the writer's time, God had spoken by a Son, that is, someone who was related to him in a way that the prophets were not. We need to say that the prophets were not related to God in this way because the rest of Hebrews, chapter 1, goes on to draw out quite how unique the Son is. In fact, the traditional reading of Hebrews 1 is that it upholds the deity of the Son in contrast to both human beings and angels.

This has an important implication for our present discussion. Since Jesus is the unique Son of God, he is in a unique position to comment on the Bible and, in particular, on whether or not the work of other prophets should be accorded greater authority than sources of knowledge outside the Bible.

This matters because if we claim we can judge what truly reveals God better than Jesus can judge, then we seem to be saying that we are closer to God than he is and, to that extent, are 'better prophets' than he is. In fact, if we do know better than Jesus what reveals God, then Jesus' work as a prophet seems redundant. He adds nothing to our understanding. After all, on this view, where we do accept what he says, this is not because he has brought us something that we do not already know, but rather he has said something that we already know and can judge is true for other reasons. Obviously this diminishes him very considerably as a prophet. We would not need him for that. Naturally, that contrasts very sharply with the way Jesus understands himself. He thinks he does bring revelation about God that we do not otherwise have (see for example what Jesus says in Matthew 11:27).

b. Jesus as the unique authoritative king

Secondly, Jesus is depicted in the New Testament as having genuine authority. In particular, he applies Psalm 110 to himself, and this psalm refers to all things being put by God under the feet of his king. God has established Jesus as our king, and tells us at the key moment of revelation in the Transfiguration to 'Listen to him' (see Mark 9:7). 'Listen' here surely carries the sense of 'obey', 'submit to' and 'learn from'.

But if we refuse to listen to what Jesus says (who actually does express the will of his Father who has made him king), then it becomes extraordinarily hard to see this as compatible with the kind of personal relationship with Jesus that the New Testament teaches. It is quite right to join in singing the hymn 'Jesus, lover of my soul,' but this recognition that Jesus loves does not exclude the aspect of authority that Jesus himself claims in his relationship both with each one of us and also with his people collectively. Thus Jesus indicates very clearly in passages such as John 15:9ff that he expects his disciples to obey him.

Of course, words like 'obey' do not necessarily play very well in a culture like ours that tends to be suspicious of authority. Indeed, part of our current suspicion is a fear that obedience and authority tend to kill real friendship and personal relationship. Our culture can only see obedience and love in 'either/or' terms, as alternatives. This means it tends to see personal relationships like this: if someone has to obey someone else, then they cannot love that person; or if someone loves somebody else, then that rules out obeying them. But when we look at John 15:9ff, we see that obedience and relationship go together: thus, in John 15:14, Jesus comments that we are his friends if we do what he commands. Personal friendship with Jesus is marked by obeying him. In fact we can go further.

Jesus' authority is a genuinely loving authority, not a selfish exploitative authority, and is vindicated as loving precisely because it is a loving and self-sacrificial authority. We see this in Mark 10:42-45, where Jesus contrasts ordinary earthly authority, which is self-serving, with his kingship, which serves his subjects. This means that if one is citing personal relationship with Jesus as a primary issue (and we should), then Jesus claims this is a personal relationship with a particular contour: it includes obedience to him as God's king. It may be more than that, but not less. That is why his decision about the kind of authority the Bible has should be final for us who love him.

In fact, as we tease out these aspects of Jesus's kingship, we realise that accepting Jesus's view of the Bible is not just a question of him as our ruling king, but also a question of whether we love him to the point of accepting his verdict about the Bible. We do not always see that our attitude to the Bible is also an index of our love for Jesus Christ. This is a point that really does search the hearts of many of us in today's Western churches. We rightly point to the wonder of personal relationship with Jesus Christ, but sometimes we appeal to the personal dimension of our relationship with him as a way of diminishing our duty to obey him, and as a way of driving a wedge between him and the Bible.

Hence as God's unique prophet and king, we should listen to how Jesus speaks about the Bible. We begin with the way that Jesus stresses in Mark 7 that it is rightly called 'the word of God'.

Questions

1. Could people tell that you love Jesus by the way that you obey him?

2. Does anything need to change so that they could tell?

9

Words *about* God and Words *of* God

Introduction

We often hear the phrase 'Word of God' used to refer to the Bible. This is very natural given that this mirrors Jesus' own descriptions. But what did he mean, and what should we mean, when we call the Bible 'the Word of God'? How does this relate to this central question of how much authority Jesus thinks the Bible has? In this Part we need to work through the consequences of Jesus using such terms and we do so by focussing on Mark 7:1-23.

1. Mark 7:1-23

Mark 7 tells us about an incident where Jesus' disciples are being criticised for their non-compliance with the traditions of the elders. This amounts to an indirect criticism of him. In this passage we find Jesus:

- Distinguishing the word of God from purely human words;

- Observing that those who have followed purely human words rather than the word of God have hearts that are far from God and worship him in vain;

- Analysing that this distance of heart is related to substituting purely human words for God's words; and

- Describing the natural output of the human heart.

Let us set the passage out in full before developing these themes at greater length.

> The Pharisees and some of the teachers of the law who had come from Jerusalem gathered round Jesus [2]and saw some of his disciples eating food with hands that were defiled, that is, unwashed. [3](The Pharisees and all the Jews do not eat unless they give their hands a ceremonial washing, holding to the tradition of the elders. [4]When they come from the market-place they do not eat unless they wash. And they observe many other traditions, such as the washing of cups, pitchers and kettles.)

> [5]So the Pharisees and teachers of the law asked Jesus, 'Why don't your disciples live according to the tradition of the elders instead of eating their food with defiled hands?'

> [6]He replied, 'Isaiah was right when he prophesied about you hypocrites; as it is written:

> '"These people honour me with their lips, but their hearts are far from me. [7]They worship me in vain; their teachings are merely human rules."

[8]'You have let go of the commands of God and are holding on to human traditions.'

[9]And he continued, 'You have a fine way of setting aside the commands of God in order to observe your own traditions! [10]For Moses said, "Honour your father and mother," and, "Anyone who curses their father or mother is to be put to death." [11]But you say that if anyone declares that what might have been used to help their father or mother is Corban (that is, devoted to God) – [12]then you no longer let them do anything for their father or mother. [13]Thus you nullify the word of God by your tradition that you have handed down. And you do many things like that.'

[14]Again Jesus called the crowd to him and said, 'Listen to me, everyone, and understand this. [15]Nothing outside a person can defile them by going into them. Rather, it is what comes out of a person that defiles them.'

[17]After he had left the crowd and entered the house, his disciples asked him about this parable. [18]'Are you so dull?' he asked. 'Don't you see that nothing that enters a person from the outside can defile them? [19]For it doesn't go into their heart but into their stomach, and then out of the body.' (In saying this, Jesus declared all foods clean.)

[20]He went on: 'What comes out of a person is what defiles them. [21]For it is from within, out of a person's heart, that evil thoughts come – sexual immorality, theft, murder, [22]adultery, greed, malice, deceit, lewdness, envy, slander, arrogance and folly. [23]All these evils come from inside and defile a person.'

2. Hypocrisy—an over-reaction?

The presenting issue here at the start of Mark chapter 7 is the way the disciples have not washed according to the tradition of the elders (v. 5). At first glance this seems an innocent enough question, and raises some concerns about the observation of tradition. But Jesus' response in verse 6a appears initially to be disproportionate. He calls these people, who appear to be highly and sincerely concerned with traditional observances, 'hypocrites'. This seems harsh at first glance. Why 'hypocrites'?

What is more, the hypocrisy charge is closely connected with what follows in verses 6b-8. He sees their behaviour as fulfilling a prophetic prediction of Isaiah that people will purport to honour God with ostensible statements of worship, but that in fact their hearts will be distant from God; so that their worship is in fact futile.

This last element of futile worship is clearly a dreadful outcome. An indispensable part of fruitful human relationship with God is worshipping him, so to be told that one's worship is futile is to be told of a profound relational estrangement that takes us away from authentic humanity.

a. The content of the charge: Leaving the commandments of God and holding to human tradition

In verse 8, Jesus begins to explain what has led to this hypocrisy and vain worship. Isaiah is addressing those who leave the commandments of God and hold to human traditions. Jesus explains why he has made this reference in verses 9-13. He has cited the Isaiah prophecy because, by their use of the humanly-devised 'Corban' rule, the Pharisees and others have devised a way to block out, or trump, the commandment to honour one's father and mother, which is drawn from the Decalogue, God's Law.

This means that the Pharisees and scribes have preferred one authority to another. They have used tradition, which comes after Moses, to trump Moses. If this was all there was to it, one would have a classic instance of one human authority being preferred to another. In contemporary thinking, justifications for this could readily spring to mind: Moses was after all a Bronze Age leader of a more or less nomadic people group, whereas later generations had more sophisticated iron technology and a more advanced social organisation, as well as more accumulated wisdom and experience to draw on. Naturally there was something to be said for preferring the traditions as against Moses. There again, there is something that sounds deeply pious about preferring something offered to God over the command to honour parents. Surely God should come first? Whatever the reason, one authority has been preferred to another.

Jesus clearly takes enormous exception to this. His point turns on the fact that this is not a simple case of preferring one human authority to another. Instead it is a case of preferring purely human words to God's word. Thus, in verse 13, Jesus summarises these activities as making void the word of God, and he says that the Pharisees do many other similar things. The Corban rule is, so to speak, the tip of the iceberg. It appears that there is a regular method at work, by which purely human words are preferred to God's words. In the end, the Pharisees and scribes obey a purely human authority at the expense of God's.

b. The real source of uncleanness
In the concluding verses of this section (vv. 17-23), Jesus draws out where uncleanness for human beings comes from. It is not something acquired from outside, but something that arises, as it were, spontaneously from within us after the Fall of humanity. It is a question of inner inclination rather than contamination from the outside.

c. The hypocrisy of chapter 7 and the treatment of God's Word
By the end of the section there is considerable clarity about Jesus' initial, apparently harsh charge of hypocrisy. He is speaking with people who seem outwardly concerned for the honour of God (for the Corban rule does sound very concerned with God's honour), but who have actually dishonoured him by the way they have treated his commands (note the way that Jesus stresses, in verse 9, that a command of God is at stake). The hypocrisy relates to the gulf between ostensible honour and real dishonour, which speaks of hearts that are not close to God, and which do not have an authentic relation of worship. The hypocrisy matters so much because it shows relational breakdown, and this relational catastrophe has arisen from how God's Word has been handled. In fact, the way God's Word is treated is a litmus test for this relational gulf.

3. The key distinction
Jesus does, after all, in this passage drive us to using terms like 'the word of God'. For him, some words really do count as 'the word of God'. He thinks that there is

a distinct category of statements that count as the Word of God. This is a limited category. That means that there are some things that do not count as the Word of God. This is essential to the point about hypocrisy and vain worship that he is making. If we think he is wrong about this, then his argument here – and elsewhere – falls to the ground. For him, there are statements that are the Word of God and statements that are not. This faces us, at its sharpest, with whether Jesus can identify better than we can what leads to futile and vain worship. If we think he cannot, then the issue is not about the authority of the Bible so much as a fundamental issue about who Jesus is.

Bluntly, if Jesus cannot identify better than us what leads to futile and vain worship, then he is not the unique prophet and he is not the kind of God-appointed king we need, since we know God and his will better than Jesus does. On the other hand, if we think Jesus really is the prophet and king he claims to be, then it follows that, as a matter of what is both right and also wise, we should accept what he says about the difference between the Word of God and purely human words.

Once this distinction that Jesus draws is borne in mind, the significance of what the scribes and Pharisees have done emerges very clearly. They have made a substitution in terms of what should be obeyed. They have exchanged purely human words as finally authoritative for God's words.

It is worth thinking through how abolishing this distinction between what is and what is not God's Word can manifest itself. Three ways immediately suggest themselves.

a. Undoing Jesus' distinction by preferring something else as authoritative rather than the Word of God

This is precisely what happens here in Mark 7. The Corban rule invented by the elders is preferred to the teaching of God. It is worth noting at this point in a little more detail how the Corban rule could theoretically be presented as a result of the kind of trajectory within the Bible that we have discussed earlier. (We are not, of course, arguing that this is how historically the rule arose.)

The trajectory could go like this. One can envisage someone looking at the sacrificial requirements of the Old Testament and noting that with things like tithing there appears to be an idea that God comes first. After all, there is a basic principle of loving God with heart, soul, mind and strength (Deut. 6:4-5). Why not extend that idea of God coming first even to material things with which one would otherwise honour one's father and mother? Surely that is an even more striking demonstration of honouring God? Would this not be going the extra mile in honouring God? However, we should note that what makes this trajectory unacceptable for Jesus is precisely that it leads to a contradiction of an express command. The trajectory – and it has a specious, pious plausibility – is not allowed to supplant an express command of God.

This example of Corban matters, we need to emphasise, because this is not an instance of purely human words expressly wanting to deny God and his honour. Rather the surface actions, as Jesus' quotation from Isaiah shows, show an apparent reverence for God and a desire to place him first. The elders have certainly been speaking about God and his honour, but, as we shall see, while they are words *about* God, they are not words *of* God.

This is a surprisingly fundamental point. By teaching that not all words about God are genuine words of God, Jesus is stating the principle of a canon of Scripture. By 'canon' here we are getting at the idea that there is a set body of texts. Because that body of texts is set and cannot be added to, it can function as a rule against which to measure other claims about God. We can start to say that something cannot be of God because it contradicts something that we know comes from him, given that it is in the canon.[1]

b. Undoing Jesus' distinction by treating nothing as the Word of God

There is another way, however, of achieving the same result that Jesus deplores, i.e. that the Word of God is not treated as such. One may not treat one's own words, or any other human's, as having a superior authority to the Bible. One may be very frank about one's limitations, but one may also so treat the Bible that it has no authority either.

The most obvious way of doing this is to deny the possibility that any word can really be the word of God, in other words that there is no such thing as inspiration or no sure way to identify what is inspired. All words in Christian faith and theology are only ever words about

---

1   Naturally, some would reply to this that this assumes God does not contradict himself. For reasons why God does not contradict himself, see later under who God is as a speaker (Ch. 10).

God, and not words of God. Alternatively, and a more current way of doing this, is to deny that we can ever be sure about what the Bible means and neither can we be sure about what other possible sources of authority mean, whether those other sources are saints of previous ages or one's own internal religious instinct.

The difficulty with both these ways of behaving is that they fall so far short of what Jesus says. Jesus is clear that there is a category we must call the Word of God and that it must be obeyed. This presupposes that God does speak (so inspiration does happen) and that what he speaks has to be listened to (so one cannot simply shrug one's shoulders and not take any action on the basis of what one thinks God's Word says). Further, Jesus is clear that he at least can tell what is a word of God and what is only a purely human word about God. This is critical. This is not just another instance of any old human being saying they can tell the difference between the Word of God and a purely human word: it is Jesus. This takes us right back to who we think he is. And if we think he is wrong about that, then, as we have said earlier, our real problem is not the authority of the Bible but our denial that Jesus is prophet and king. Jesus is clear that God does speak. These considerations will take us to the highly significant question of what kind of speaker God will be.

This is not, naturally, to say that no passage of the Bible is difficult to understand. Some passages clearly are. But in the light of what Jesus says, we must be careful about allowing ourselves to become paralysed when trying to apply the Word of God on the grounds that complete and infallible certainty about our interpretations is not possible.

c. Undoing Jesus' distinction by treating too many things as the Word of God

The final way in which we can undo the distinction that Jesus draws is by simply asserting that God's Word is indeed authoritative, but that it is an authority that we must employ alongside all other legitimate authorities. Favourite candidates here for being alternative sources of authority on the same level as the Bible are human reason and tradition. There again, as we have earlier seen, the believer's heart guided by the Spirit has been asserted as such a source, and also the inner instinct of anyone, since the divine light dwells in all human beings.

It is worth trying to be precise with what is happening here. The issue is not whether reason, tradition, conscience or the Spirit-guided heart have contributions to make to our thinking. The issue is how much authority these sources have, and how much weight their contributions carry. We referred above to the way that in this passage Jesus introduces in principle the idea of a canon of Scripture. And the implication of what Jesus says is that these other things are not necessarily to be taken as God's Word so that if we put these alongside God's Word, then we do not allow his Word to function as it should.

If we did put these other claims alongside God's Word, we would, in fact, have made a judgment that we can discern an equal authority in these other sources of knowledge. We would be implying that we can tell what is of God, and what is not, without his Word telling us. In particular we would again be suggesting that our spiritual judgment about what is, or is not, pleasing to God is better than Jesus's. As we have seen, that is fraught with problems about who we then think Jesus is, not just what we think the Bible is.

4. Why does Jesus make this distinction?

Yet the next question is this: why does Jesus make such a sharp distinction? The distinction is basically all about origin: where the words in question come from. Thus the Corban rule comes from the elders and it is a tradition that they have created and fostered. The commandment to honour father and mother is one of the Ten Commandments and was given by God to Moses. This question of origin helps us understand why it is that not all words about God are equal, no matter how clever or saintly the people who think them up. The reason why some words about God are special is that they originate with him. They are his words about himself, not just a human being's best words about him. We stress again, not all words about God are words of God. God actually chooses some words to describe himself and to express his will for us.

It is important to add here that when Jesus calls the command to honour father and mother the Word of God, he does so in the full knowledge that Moses was involved in the revelation of the Ten Commandments to Israel. He refers in Mark 7:10 to Moses's role. This matters because of what is sometimes called dual authorship. Jesus' account here recognises a human dimension in Moses, but his emphasis lies on God as originator.

This takes us to a key consideration. We can see that Jesus is making his distinction between two kinds of words about God, words which are of God and words which are purely human, and once we see this and realise that this is a distinction based on origin, we see this distinction turns on who the speaker is in each case, the Word of God and a purely human word. Ultimately Jesus makes the distinction he does because with the Word of God it is God who speaks. This means we must now turn to the implications of having God as a speaker.

Questions

In this chapter we have been stressing the distinction Jesus draws between the Word of God and purely human words. We need to try and apply this:

- Can you think of instances where you or your church have undone that distinction by taking something else as authoritative rather than the Word of God?

- Can you think of instances where you or your church have effectively treated nothing as the Word of God?

- Can you think of instances where you or your church have treated too many things as the Word of God?

Going deeper #2
Dual authorship: A partnership of equals?

Rightly understood, dual authorship is an important and fruitful idea for the Christian reader of the Bible. Dual authorship suggests that both God and an ordinary human being are involved in any part of the Bible. Unlike in some other religions, in Christian belief the Word of God is not given on supernatural paper with supernatural writings that men and women then read and copy, with or without supernatural reading glasses.

Instead, God works congruently with, say, John the apostle in writing the Gospel, so that the Gospel of John really does have John's own voice and style. John's personality is not obliterated.[2] Dual authorship helps explain why so many different tones and voices can genuinely be heard in the Bible.

Dual authorship also means that we must be alive to the human component to any particular part of the Bible. Thus, when you read something by John, it helps to know how much he likes to make ironic points (as in the trial sequence before Pilate), or construct sections using a chain of themes which lead on from one to another (as in the discussion on who is the real 'father' of those Jesus is talking to in John 8:31-59).

We also have to ask how the divine and human elements interrelate, however. Is the human element so strong that it limits God in what he can say, such that he cannot say what he really means? Perhaps even more importantly, does it limit God morally, so that the human element sullies or contaminates what God says, as when perhaps a co-writer who is racist brings some of his own prejudice and sin into a collaborative writing project with someone who is not? In more colloquial terms, is God brought down to the level and limits, intellectual and moral, of his human co-author?

These kinds of questions occur in any writing 'partnership': in a sense, one is asking if there is a 'senior partner' in a particular writing 'partnership'. Thus we can envisage a joint writing project between a senior academic and a junior one, in which the most significant insights flow primarily from the senior, and the particular book has a place in an over-arching scheme that the senior academic can see quite clearly and the junior much less so.

We turn back now to the way Jesus handles the question of both Moses and God being involved in the giving of the Ten Commandments. For Jesus there is a primacy to God's involvement in the giving of the law about parents.

For the important thing, when it comes to the question of authority, is not that Moses is better than the elders, but that God has spoken in the Ten Commandments. The comparison is not of one human with

---

2   On occasions, God does directly dictate a particular message: e.g. the letters to the seven churches in Revelation 2–3, where the refrain is 'to the angel of the church in … write …'

another human, but of humans with God. Thus Jesus does not deny the presence of Moses in the giving of the Ten Commandments, but the key thing is the way God originates the Ten Commandments.

This is, of course, perfectly intelligible. If two human authors co-operate – one of whom is an unknown, while the other is a hugely significant and respected figure – one readily understands why attention may focus on the significant figure rather than on the unknown. The weight of what is written readily comes in this kind of dual authorship from the 'senior' partner in the relationship. It is a question of who the senior partner is, and who the unknown one is.

This means that when we assert – rightly – the dual authorship of the Bible, we are asserting that both human and divine 'contributions' are important, but we are not asserting that they are of equal importance when it comes to authority. Jesus is clear that the divine side trumps any alternative claim to authority. Nor are we asserting that the divine side is limited or frustrated by the human author with whom God works.

This latter point is more important than we might first think. Let us imagine for a moment that we disagreed with it and said that the human side of dual authorship is indeed so significant that in fact God cannot express himself as accurately, or with as much purity, as he wishes.

If we took this position then we would be saying in principle that human sin and limitation did affect God so that he could not always achieve what he wished. If that were so, then God is a good deal more limited in terms of his promises both to us for our salvation and also to Jesus, to establish him as eternal king. The limitation on God's sovereignty that we would be conceding on this argument cannot be confined to the Bible and the revelation of God alone: it also affects the certainty of our salvation. But if we think, as we must, that God's promise of salvation is certain and utterly trustworthy, then we are saying something about his words and should work that through consistently with regard to all that he says.

To this extent we need to say again that dual authorship is telling us there are two authors, not that there are two equal authors, let alone that the human side predominates.

10

When God Speaks

Introduction

Think of those moments when you see a televised debate between politicians just before an election. Say that the subject is the economy. We very readily find we start to weigh them up as speakers. And the most significant things are not how they look or whether they have a regional accent, but a range of factors. After all, when seriously evaluating any speaker we normally look at a number of qualities in them:

- Their knowledge. (Do they know the truth in order to be able to tell it, and tell it coherently? If we think the politician knows nothing about the economy, we rate them lower.)

- Their ethical character. (Do they have a character that will speak the truth? We think back to remember whether a politician has kept promises.)

- Their effectiveness. (Do their words have effect? What power do their words have to shape reality? What is the politician promising to do? Can it be done by them, or by anyone?)

1. God as a unique speaker

When we ask these questions about God as speaker, we have to remember the way that, throughout the Bible, he constantly differentiates himself both from ordinary human speakers and from false gods, from idols.

a. God's knowledge and speaking the future

In particular, God claims uniqueness in the way that he alone can speak the future. This emerges with great clarity in Isaiah 48, in a section of the book where the uniqueness of God as against idols and humanity is constantly underlined.

'Listen to this, you descendants of Jacob,
    you who are called by the name of Israel
    and come from the line of Judah,
you who take oaths in the name of the Lord
    and invoke the God of Israel –
    but not in truth or righteousness –
²you who call yourselves citizens of the holy city
    and claim to rely on the God of Israel –
    the Lord Almighty is his name:
³I foretold the former things long ago,
    my mouth announced them and I made them known;
    then suddenly I acted, and they came to pass.
⁴For I knew how stubborn you were;
    your neck muscles were iron,
    your forehead was bronze.
⁵Therefore I told you these things long ago;

> before they happened I announced them to you
> so that you could not say,
> > "My images brought them about;
> > my wooden image and metal god ordained them."
> ⁶You have heard these things; look at them all.
> > Will you not admit them?
>
> 'From now on I will tell you of new things,
> > of hidden things unknown to you.
> ⁷They are created now, and not long ago;
> > you have not heard of them before today.
> So you cannot say,
> > "Yes, I knew of them."'

What emerges very strongly here is that the ability to foretell the future marks God out. In particular, verse 7 makes it clear that such foretelling is not the kind of knowledge that human beings can have.

The reason for such an ability is not far to seek. God, in his Old Testament polemic against idols, repeatedly states that idols are created while he is not, and that idols do not create while he does (see Jer. 10:1-16). As the uncreated creator of all he is able to know all, both what is in creation and also himself.

With regard to creation, he knows everything about what is in it, since he created it. Nor can we argue that God is unaware of what he has created, as if the cosmos, as it were, grew out of him unknown to himself in the way that my hair may grow without my being aware of it. The reason why God is completely aware of his creation is that it exists and is sustained by his will and intention (Rev. 4:11) and according to his word (see Gen. 1 and 2).

But as well as knowing exhaustively the cosmos he has created, God is also in a position to know himself exhaustively. Since he is uncreated there is no past that is unknown to him. We as creatures, by contrast, are limited in terms of direct knowledge of ourselves since by definition we have a beginning in time. For us, there is therefore a past before we began to exist to which we have no direct access. That past, however, contributes to who we are, and if we wish to know ourselves fully and in depth, we have to reckon with the history that pre-dates us but still affects us. With regard to the future, a creature exists in time and is limited by experiencing time successively, moment by moment. There is knowledge about myself that will become available to me that I do not currently have. Because I experience things, including myself, successively, moment by moment, I do not know myself fully. Parts of my history and my knowledge of them lie in my future: I do not know all of myself all the time.

God, however, is not limited by time in this kind of way and is therefore able to know the future even as well as he knows the present and past. Older theologians used to say that God knows all things, past, present and future in one single act of knowing (simultaneous from our viewpoint). Equally, he knows all of himself all of the time; he is not handicapped by growing in self-knowledge over time.

Thus, as we unpack how God can speak the future, we see how this is connected with the way that he is unique, the uncreated creator of all, and able to tell the truth because he knows everything within the cosmos he created, past, present and future. As creator of all, he knows every item within the cosmos: he knows its past, present and future. He knows it in its immediate relations round about it, and he knows it in relation to all other things, no matter how apparently distant. He knows each thing in itself and in all its relationships and context, no matter how broad. He knows his cosmos – collectively and in its individuality – exhaustively. Equally, as uncreated, he knows himself exhaustively. All this means that God is in a position to tell the truth authoritatively because he knows it completely. Moreover, he can tell the truth coherently because he understands all things in their true relation to each other and to him. He can exhaustively comprehend what he is talking about. Nobody else can talk like this, because nobody else is the uncreated creator of all.

Of course, one possible objection might be that while the Old Testament understands God's knowledge this way, it is not how the New Testament does. This, though, is to understate the place that Jesus gives predictive prophecy. For example, the words of Jesus in Mark 7 see the quotation from Isaiah precisely as a predictive prophecy that is being fulfilled. Similarly Jesus regards his own Passion in the light of fulfilment of prophecy. For these reasons, we have to say that Jesus thinks God's knowledge extends to future events and this underlines the uniqueness of God's knowledge.

b. God's ethical character and speaking

Naturally the next question is this: Even if God does exhaustively know the truth about himself and his cosmos, does he have the ethical character to tell the truth?

In terms of Jesus' understanding, he is clear that God is good and perfect (see for example Matt. 5:48). This naturally ties both to Abraham's understanding that God as God of all the earth must do right (Gen. 18:25) and to Paul's statement that God does not lie (Titus 1:2). But perhaps even more significantly, the truthfulness of God's words has to be taken with the major biblical theme of God's covenant faithfulness: God is a God who keeps his promises. If we think God is not truthful as a character, then we would have to conclude that his promises are not sure and trustworthy. But the theme of God's trustworthiness is persistent and critical: from the provision of offspring to Abraham, the deliverance from Egypt (God 'remembers' his covenant) through to the cries of joy surrounding the births of John the Baptist and Jesus, God's people respond to the effect that God has kept his covenant promises of salvation (see Luke 1–2).

God's moral character, however, needs to be taken more broadly than just trustworthiness and faithfulness. Conventional Christian teaching is that he is completely good and holy; in fact, morally perfect in every way. This is important because his ethical character as a speaker is not just one who tells the truth, but one whose words will be good. The point is, that if God is perfectly and ethically good, he will never speak evil, but his words will always be good.

This, though, is a radically challenging thought for some in our churches today. Concerns have been variously raised about racism and genocide in the Old Testament, while the New Testament has been perceived as, amongst other things, sexist and homophobic, and at times anti-Semitic. On occasion, this is politely put as being a product of the limitations of the human writers, but unmistakably, even if these qualities are tactfully attributed to the human side of the divine/human dual authorship, moral evaluations have been made which see these words as ethically bad or immoral.

Yet there is an obvious problem here. Quite clearly the Bible does not understand itself as being morally imperfect or limited. Thus Psalm 19:7-10 celebrates precisely the perfection of God's law or Word, and verse 11 goes on to note the way that God's Word can correct our understanding. One might add that Psalm 119 is a prolonged reflection on the value of God's Word and listening to it. Again, this does not suggest limitation or imperfection.

But if these passages that we find so difficult really are from God who is perfectly good, then we would have to say that they are good and that it is our perceptions of what counts as good and bad that need to change. It is, after all, a basic but important thought that the Bible is meant to provide correction to how we think about various things. Of course, at this point some may want to say that they still think the passages in question are bad and that they are simply not the Word of God. This, though, faces some of the great difficulties we have looked at earlier. First, it ends up treating the Bible very differently from the way Jesus says we should, because it refuses to treat certain passages as being God's words. Secondly, it ends up with a God who cannot say what he wants to say, given the fatal limitations of his human co-authors.

This question of the goodness of God's Word is worth putting in a wider context. Genesis 1 and 2 describes the creation of the world with some repeated refrains, One of them, of course, is that God speaks, and it is so, and another is that God looks at what he has created, and it is good. A final motif is the way God speaks blessing on his creation. In that way the creation narrative consistently underlines the goodness of what God speaks. By contrast, denying that what God says is good is something that Adam and Eve do by necessary implication in Genesis 3, as they accept the lies of the serpent which suggest that God's Word of Genesis 2:17 is not true and is morally flawed, since it is given in envy rather than benevolence and kindness.

We have again reached a critical point which relates to trust and to faith. Christians are those who have faith in God's promises of salvation. If we do say that God does not tell the truth always, or cannot express himself properly, what happens to his promises of salvation? We would surely have to conclude that they are not ultimately reliable and that, in prudence, we should plan to work for our own salvation. Strikingly, this would introduce an attitude that Jesus does not share: he clearly, albeit with struggle and tears, does trust that his Father will keep his promises to him, both to raise him from the dead and to provide a kingdom for him. The gospels testify that Jesus trusts God to be faithful—which involves God being truthful.

c. The power of God's speaking

The final area relating to God's Word is whether it is effective or not. After all, a word may be uttered, and uttered by someone with sound knowledge and good intentions, but that word can be frustrated by others intervening to stop it having effect. Put another way, how sovereign is God's Word? Can people stop his Word bearing the fruit he intends?

It is useful here to pick up a further thread from Isaiah. Isaiah prophesies (in chapter 55:10-11):

As the rain and the snow
   come down from heaven,
and do not return to it
   without watering the earth
and making it bud and flourish,
   so that it yields seed for the sower and bread for the
eater,
so is my word that goes out from my mouth:
   it will not return to me empty,
but will accomplish what I desire
   and achieve the purpose for which I sent it.

These words are uttered in the context of God's promise to provide an everlasting covenant and forgiveness of sin. This reminds us that there is a close connection between the reliability of God's promises of salvation and his sovereignty or ability to carry his word out. In particular, the forgiveness of our sins is related to what God promises. The point made in Isaiah here is that God's word will be effective for what he intends. The question therefore for any word of God in any particular situation is what God intends for it in that situation. One cannot say that God's word 'fails' if by that one means that he intends to achieve something and then fails to do so. This again takes us to Jesus' reliance on his Father's ability to fulfil the promises he had made in his Son.

The effectiveness of God's word again looks obvious after one has considered the Genesis narrative of chapters 1 and 2. The most repeated refrain is that God speaks and it is so. It is not so much that God's word corresponds to reality, but rather that the reality of the cosmos corresponds to God's word. In fact the cosmos is completely dependent on God's word and will.

Conclusion: a perfect speaker brings perfect words

Taken together, this establishes that the God who speaks God's word knows the truth completely and coherently, speaks what is truthful and good because he is truthful and good, and is able to speak effectively, because he tells us his word will achieve what he intends for it. Further since God himself is incomparably greater than anything within creation, the words he speaks will be incomparably greater too.

Hence there is nothing absurd in seeing God's Word as coherent and consistent: he has the knowledge, ethical character and effectiveness to ensure this is so. In fact, these attributes of God do give force and explanation to how it is that Psalm 19:7ff can speak of the perfection of God's Word. Again, this is part of the standard beliefs of earlier theologians who would write of the 'perfection' of the Bible. Richard Hooker is quite typical when he writes:

> God himself can neither possibly err, nor lead into error. For this cause his testimonies, whatsoever he affirmeth, are always truth and most infallible certainty. Yea further, because the things that proceed from him are perfect without any manner of defect or maim; it cannot be but that the words of his mouth are absolute, and lack nothing which they should have for performance of that thing whereunto they tend.[1]

---

1   Richard Hooker, *Of the Laws of Ecclesiastical Polity* II.VI.1

In this quotation, Hooker's statements about what the Bible is really hang on who he thinks God is. Since he thinks God is perfect, it follows that his words which comprise promises will be perfect too. As such, Christian faith and trust follow perfectly naturally and reasonably. But if we say that those words are not perfect, then equally our faith and trust be misplaced: God's words would not be trustworthy enough.

This in turn establishes how disastrous it is to substitute God's Word for anything less. Not only is it using immeasurably inferior sources of information, but it is also profoundly dishonouring to God, for it suggests that purely human words can in some circumstances be somehow better than God's, either ethically, or in terms of truth, or in terms of effect. It is no wonder, then, that Jesus reacts so strongly to substituting purely human words for God's words.

But, of course, is it the case that purely human words are so defective? This takes us to the question of who we are.

Questions

In ordinary human communication, it makes a difference when we really know and understand the people that we're talking to. Please read Psalm 139 and think through/discuss this question: 'Does God know me well enough to talk to me?'

11

When We Speak

Introduction

Think back to the example we used earlier of the TV debate between politicians, and how we as viewers or audience have to weigh up what those politicians are like. But now expand it a little, and think of the questions that come back at those politicians from the studio audience, and think of it also from the politicians' point of view. They have to think about the audience that is asking them questions: what lies behind the questions? When a questioner claims to have an expertise, is that true? As the politician answers, what is the questioner hearing? And is he or she hearing the politician fairly?

The reason we are citing this further example is that we sometimes have to ask not just what one particular speaker is like, but what several are like and what the people are like who are listening to them and weighing them up. Just imagine: if you are a politician who really does know about the economy and global banking, it must be pretty galling to be told you're an idiot by a thick-as-a-brick studio questioner who failed G.C.S.E. economics. You may feel that person is in no position to judge.

Applying that here, as we think about the whole question of God's words and purely human words, we have to ask not just who God is, but who we are. That question of who we are, just like the questioner from the studio audience, affects both what we say and how we listen. Accordingly we need to look at both these dimensions: first, what kind of speakers we ourselves are; and secondly, what kind of listeners we are.

1. Who we are as speakers

After his scathing description, in Mark 7, of the way the Scribes and Pharisees had substituted purely human words for God's Word, Jesus goes on to explain his comments in the context of uncleanness.

We remember that the dispute started with objections from the Pharisees and Scribes over uncleanness, and the perceived need to be cleansed from things from outside that make a person unclean. When Jesus returns to the issue of uncleanness, he explains that uncleanness is not something that comes in from outside to make what was previously clean unclean. Rather uncleanness is already there within a human being. Jesus specifies several different kinds of uncleanness which defile a person and which are endemic in the human heart. Some of these are obvious enough—sexual immorality, greed and violence. But we must also note the presence of sins of the tongue. Part of the uncleanness that dwells within the human heart is that we are dishonest speakers—something that is of course addressed in the Ten Commandments, as are so many of the activities that Jesus cites here.

Now, this is not to say that all people are as dishonest as they could possibly be, all the time, in everything that they say. It is worth remembering with regard to the prohibition on false testimony in the Ten Commandments that we can achieve at least some honesty some of the time, just as we can achieve at least an outer conformity to the prohibitions on murder, theft and adultery. The difficulty is the perfect obedience of which Jesus speaks in the Sermon on the Mount. But the fact that dishonest speech is part of the fruit of our hearts means that our words are correspondingly less reliable. Even in human affairs we rightly say that one person is more honest than another. And if we know someone can be highly prone to dishonesty we discount their speech accordingly.

This means that even though not every word we say is a lie, there is a fatal disadvantage in giving unconditional acceptance to a purely human word. We are simply not that reliable as speakers. A human speaker does not always tell the truth and so his or her promises are not as trustworthy as God's. This is not just in terms of the ability to keep promises, but of the moral character to want to do so. This in turn underlines the tragic folly of substituting the words of the elders for God's Word given through Moses. It is preferring the liar to the truth-teller.

This moral problem is compounded by the other factors we noted above about weighing whether a speaker should be listened to, namely knowledge and the ability to perform what one says. With regard to knowledge, since we are creatures existing in time and space, and are limited by those dimensions in what we can know, we simply do not know as much as God. Indeed, even what we do know is limited as regards of context, since we cannot know each thing in relation to all other things. Further, with regard to the ability to perform what we say, our finitude limits the worth of our speech. We cannot always make reality conform to our words. Our words and promises can be frustrated despite our best plans and intentions. These various considerations of our finitude provide further reasons for valuing purely human words as less than God's. He simply knows more and can make things happen. Why substitute flawed and ineffective purely human words for God's?

All this, though, inevitably raises the question of why we accept human words, given what human beings are like as speakers.

2. Who we are as hearers

The issues of uncleanness to which Jesus points in Mark 7 do not simply impact us as speakers. If indeed I have an unclean heart that is defiled with immorality, greed and fatal violence, then this will affect me as a hearer too.

It will mean on the one hand that I have a desperate need to hear truly-spoken words about what I should do and how I may be cleansed. For Jesus' description of my unclean heart shows how much I need to hear the truth about these things for which I sinfully long. But on the other hand, the very fact that I long for these things suggests that I will be slow sometimes to hear the truth that such desires are present in me, that they are sinful, and that I am inwardly unclean.

The unclean heart that Jesus describes therefore has a terrible problem that has a dual aspect. On the one hand, it needs the very thing that it will, on the other hand, be inclined to reject: truthful words about God and his will. This suggests that we should have a certain attitude, or hermeneutics, of suspicion, not so much towards the Bible (for being suspicious of God is deeply problematic and hints at arrogance towards him), but towards ourselves as people who hear God's Word. By 'hermeneutics of suspicion' here I am getting at the idea that we interpret and listen to what someone says bearing in mind that they may be trying to deceive, are biased, or are just plain ignorant.

The implication of Jesus' words in Mark 7 about our hearts, then, is not a naïve dismissal of the hermeneutics, or interpretative stance, of suspicion. Its correct application is towards a more sophisticated and nuanced attitude of suspicion. In fact, it takes the hermeneutics of suspicion further. It does encourage us to remember that human speakers may be deceitful and that it is therefore appropriate to ask, 'Does he or she have an interest or hidden agenda in telling me this?' That is, if you like, a perfectly normal hermeneutics or stance of suspicion. But with regard to the Word of God, it encourages a different question, one regarding us as readers or hearers of his Word: 'Why would I like God to have said something different here?' We start to suspect ourselves as hearers. It is just here that a biblical hermeneutics of suspicion along the lines Jesus encourages is both more sophisticated and farther reaching. It is certainly more uncomfortable for us to ask ourselves these questions as hearers. But it is also much more consistent, and much more honest.

Given that all this is so in Genesis 3, why would we assume that our own hearing could competently judge by itself what is or is not God's Word, or what is consistent with it? The answer is that we could make no such assumption because of the huge risks that we would be simply protecting the inclinations of our unclean hearts.

In Mark 7, Jesus' distinction between words of God and purely human words creates a choice of brutal simplicity for us. If we have an approach to the Bible that does not treat it as fully God's Word, then we have by implication decided that there is some source of knowledge which enables us to make that judgment, and that that source of knowledge is better than Jesus. To this extent, Jesus urges us to have no substitutes either for the Word of God, or indeed for him as God's ultimate prophet.

With this in mind we move next to charting what is involved for Jesus in treating the Word of God as the Word of God.

Questions

Please read Psalm 146:3-4 and think through/discuss the following questions:

- What is wrong with trusting 'princes'?

- Who counts as 'princes' for us?

Going deeper #3
'We can't go on together, with suspicious minds'

This discussion about suspicion matters greatly because understanding of suspicion has become such a major approach to interpreting the Bible in recent years. The thinking behind this is that, as readers, we must come to anything we read with suspicion, bearing in mind that the writer comes from a particular social and historical location, has his or her own interests to defend or advocate, and so on. Thus when we read an account of the life and culture of an indigenous population which was written in the eighteenth century by someone from a European nation looking for places to colonise, we bear that setting in mind. We feel justified in suspecting that the writer may exaggerate social practices that Europeans think bad, but minimise or not mention at all any positive accomplishments on the part of the indigenous population. As readers we feel justified in being suspicious and looking for gaps in what an author writes. What is more, we may feel an obligation to do this, reading, as it were, on behalf of those who have been silenced or not represented by the author in question. We feel we are doing justice for the silenced.

As we have said, this interpretative stance of suspicion has been applied to the Bible, notably with regard to its alleged sexism and, for some New Testament writers, their alleged anti-Semitism. In the case of purely human words, this hermeneutics of suspicion surely has a place. Apart from anything else it is a practical recognition, albeit an unknowing one, of what Jesus says about the human heart in Mark 7, that we are unreliable speakers. We are, after all, imperfect both because we are finite and because our moral character is fallen. Hence, as a rule of thumb it is responsible to read with due suspicion.

The question, though, is not whether a hermeneutics of suspicion is apt for reading purely human words, but whether it is right for us as readers or hearers to practise such an approach of suspicion to God's words, bearing in mind who he is as a speaker.

Apart from anything else, the dangers of an inappropriate hermeneutics of suspicion are plain in Genesis 3. Adam and Eve are led by the serpent to doubt the truth of what God says in Genesis 2:17 when he prohibits the taking of the fruit of the tree of the knowledge of good and evil on pain of death. They are led to doubt both that this is true ('you will not surely die': Genesis 3:4) and also to doubt that what God says is good (the prohibition was given because 'God knows that ... you will be like God': Genesis 3:5). From one point of view, the serpent is inviting Adam and Eve to practise an utterly classic attitude of suspicion: the speaker may not be telling the truth; and further, the speaker may only have said what he said to protect his own power and interests at the expense of the hearers. Adam and Eve accept this hermeneutics of suspicion towards God's Word, as given in Genesis 2:17.

Unfortunately, from another point of view, they have in fact not used a hermeneutics of suspicion. Thus they have not asked whether what the serpent has told them is true, and have not asked whether it says what it says out of malice toward God and them. To that extent, they have not been suspicious of the serpent. Nor have they exercised any suspicion towards themselves, for they have not asked themselves whether they want to accept what the serpent says because they have been led into pride and envy by having the prospect of 'being like God' dangled before their eyes. They should be suspicious both of the serpent as a speaker and also of themselves as hearers.

There is therefore a double tragedy about the hermeneutics of suspicion as we see it practised in Genesis 3. Suspicion is directed at the wrong person—for in Genesis 1 and 2 we know that God's words are truthful and good. And suspicion is not directed at the right people, namely the malicious speaker, the serpent, and the envious and all too self-interested hearers, Adam and Eve. The result of this misdirected and self-serving hermeneutics of suspicion is that Adam and Eve listen to someone else's words (the serpent's) instead of the words of the very speaker that Genesis 1 and 2 show to be ultimately trustworthy.

It is vital to grasp the irony here. At its best, the hermeneutics of suspicion in its right place can help stop me as a reader or hearer from being taken in and deceived by others. But in Genesis 3, the wrong hermeneutics of suspicion does not protect Adam and Eve from deception—it leads them right into it.

12

The Obedient Son

Introduction

In the previous section we have dealt with the way Jesus sees a distinction between God's Word and purely human words. But the next question is what goes into treating God's Word as his Word. Again we need to look at Jesus. At various points in the New Testament Jesus is presented as the new Adam, the man who does what the first Adam did not, and who lived a life of perfect relationship with his heavenly Father. Certainly the perfection of Jesus' life is one of the things that is underlined at his trial, as the gospel writers draw out that, in fact, Jesus is innocent of any wrong-doing. If we had any doubt about that, that is removed by the way that God raises him from the dead. Jesus' resurrection vindicates him. This means that, amongst other things, Jesus exemplifies for us a human life in which God's Word is treated rightly.

In the material we survey we shall see that Jesus thinks God's Word is necessary, to be obeyed, to be utterly trusted, is coherent around him in particular, and must be interpreted rightly.

1. Baptism and Temptation

We begin with the baptism and temptation in Matthew's Gospel (in chapters 3 and 4). These incidents are right at the start of Jesus' ministry and give a shape and direction to what follows. They need, as we shall see, to be taken together because the theme of sonship runs through both.

Before we go to the text itself, however, we need to pause at the magnitude of the temptation. Here is Jesus the man facing Satan the tempter alone, with unmistakable echoes of Genesis 3. While temptations are described or implied frequently throughout the Bible, this face to face confrontation between a human being and Satan is truly exceptional. In fact, the obvious precursor to Jesus' experience here is exactly that of Adam and Eve in Eden. Since Matthew has stressed a virgin birth for Jesus, there is a powerful sense of new beginnings as Jesus comes to John the Baptist as an adult: what will this 'new' man be like? In the temptation, we find that Jesus will stand in this face to face confrontation with Satan where Adam had fallen. To this extent, there is a genuine note of victory as Jesus resists Satan's temptations and deception. This is something underlined by theologians of the early Church, like Irenaeus of Lyons, who point out that Jesus' victory begins here in the temptation, and it is a victory of obedience to God's Word. It really matters that we grasp this dimension. Sometimes you hear the comment that 'might is right'. The victory of Jesus is not just a victory of might. Rather it is a triumph of might and right. And the right in question is the righteousness of obedience.

With this in mind, we turn to the text.

3:13Then Jesus came from Galilee to the Jordan to be baptised by John. 14But John tried to deter him, saying, 'I need to be baptised by you, and do you come to me?'

15Jesus replied, 'Let it be so now; it is proper for us to do this to fulfil all righteousness.' Then John consented.

16As soon as Jesus was baptised, he went up out of the water. At that moment heaven was opened, and he saw the Spirit of God descending like a dove and alighting on him. 17And a voice from heaven said, 'This is my Son, whom I love; with him I am well pleased.'

4:1Then Jesus was led by the Spirit into the wilderness to be tempted by the devil. 2After fasting for forty days and forty nights, he was hungry. 3The tempter came to him and said, 'If you are the Son of God, tell these stones to become bread.'

4Jesus answered, 'It is written: "Man shall not live on bread alone, but on every word that comes from the mouth of God."'

5Then the devil took him to the holy city and had him stand on the highest point of the temple. 6'If you are the Son of God,' he said, 'throw yourself down. For it is written:

> '"He will command his angels concerning you,
>   and they will lift you up in their hands,
> so that you will not strike your foot against a stone."'

7Jesus answered him, 'It is also written: "Do not put the Lord your God to the test."'

⁸Again, the devil took him to a very high mountain and showed him all the kingdoms of the world and their splendour. ⁹'All this I will give you,' he said, 'if you will bow down and worship me.'

¹⁰Jesus said to him, 'Away from me, Satan! For it is written: "Worship the Lord your God, and serve him only."'

¹¹Then the devil left him, and angels came and attended him.

The theme of sonship unites the baptism and temptation. Let us see how.

a. The promise of sonship

There is much to be said about the baptism of Jesus and what it means, but here we need to focus on the climax of the baptism, which is the voice from heaven and the words that it says. The voice from heaven identifies Jesus as God's Son, in terms which recall Psalm 2:7, where he addresses his Son. In other words, the voice from heaven is designating Jesus as the Son spoken of in Psalm 2.

Psalm 2, though, has all kinds of associations. Notably, in it God addresses his Son and makes promises to him. Those promises are for a dominion that encompasses the whole of the human world (Ps. 2:8). He is to be the cosmic king. This is the inheritance that God the Father promises to provide for his Son. After all, in biblical thought fathers do provide inheritance for their sons.

This means that the reader turns from the baptism of Jesus with God's promises of cosmic kingship for his beloved Son fresh in the mind. The baptism includes a wonderful designation of Jesus as Son, with accompanying promises of splendid inheritance. Then comes the temptation.

b. *The temptation and sonship*

Satan's temptation starts with the sonship of Jesus: 'If you are the son of God ...' (see verses 3 and 6). Satan begins with sonship, the very point that God has just confirmed in the baptism. By starting here and connecting Jesus' sonship both with having food miraculously provided, and also with having spectacular public confirmation, Satan is asking Jesus to take advantage in some sense of what God has said, yet at the same time subtly undermining it. The implication is that somehow there is doubt about whether Jesus really is the Son of God and whether he completely believes it. Accordingly Jesus needs to take God up on it, as it were.

There is in fact a two-fold undermining that is taking place here. First, the insinuation is that Jesus is perhaps not really the Son of God, which is an undermining of Jesus and his identity. Secondly, there is the further insinuation that what God has said is not completely reliable and therefore Jesus had better confirm it: God's mere word is not enough; something more is needed to show that God is serious. Here the point is that God as Father is not entirely trustworthy on his word alone.

The undermining of Jesus as God's Son, and of the worth of God's word in identifying Jesus as God's Son, continues in the last climactic temptation in Matthew's account. In chapter 4:8 Satan offers Jesus all the kingdoms of the world if he will worship Satan. Vitally, Satan is therefore offering Jesus the same inheritance that God is promising him in Psalm 2. In one way, Satan is offering to be a surrogate father to Jesus, providing him with an inheritance that is every bit as extensive as the one that he has been promised under the terms of Psalm 2. One dimension of this final temptation is that Jesus must choose who will be his 'father', providing him with an inheritance. Both putative fathers are making promises, and those promises are, in one sense, of equal extent. Jesus' choice is governed, though, not by who is making the more extensive promises of inheritance, but by what is ethically right: he cannot righteously accept Satan's promises on the terms on which he offers them.[1] Accordingly, he chooses to believe what God says rather than what Satan says, in sharp contrast to Adam and Eve. As many have noted, Jesus' response to Satan is marked by the way God's Word impacts him, and to this we now turn.

2. Necessity

To begin with, Jesus responds to Satan's first temptation (Matt. 4:3) with the quotation that human beings need God's Word as much as they need physical bread (4:4). Since physical bread is a fundamental necessity of life, Jesus is indicating that God's Word is a basic necessity. This immediately dispenses with the idea that the Bible is simply one of a number of sources of knowledge and that, provided we have been nourished by one or another, then all will be well. Rather, Jesus' point is that without God's Word, a human being starves.

The vice of Satan's suggestion, then, is that his focus on physical bread has implied that this is all that is

---

1   Naturally we may well doubt that Satan is either willing or able to keep his promises of inheritance, but that is not the point put before us in Matthew. Jesus' obedience to God's word is the point.

needed for full human life. Instead, God provides physical sustenance (in Satan's temptation, God is envisaged as the giver of bread via his angels) but also, and just as fundamentally, God gives his Word. There is therefore more to Jesus' relationship as Son of God than just being able to call on his Father for physical food.

The obvious question therefore for Christians reading this today is whether God's Word has been treated as being as fundamentally necessary, as Jesus does here, or whether it has become in some way more of an optional extra. Of course, this may not be put in quite that way. But the question is one of practice: in our services, is the Word of God treated as an absolute necessity? In the way that people are taught in our churches, and in the way that someone is instructed in our churches, is it actually the Word of God that is central, or the imperative to entertain?

3. Obedience

The next point that emerges is the stress on obedience. Jesus is concerned to obey God's Word. Thus the second temptation and the third are resisted on the basis that God has issued a command and that command must be obeyed. Hence Jesus will not 'put … God to the test', nor will he worship someone other than God. At its simplest, if we want to treat God's Word in the way that Jesus does, then we will obey it. This, after all, is a hallmark of Jesus' ministry and his final journey to Jerusalem. He goes to a place of acute danger and hostility, not just suspecting, but positively believing, that this will cost him his life. He regards himself as under a divine necessity, despite what it means for him. This readiness for a costly obedience is clearest, perhaps, in his prayers in the garden of Gethsemane where he prefers his Father's will even over his own (Mark 14:36).

Again this is a very testing question for Christians today. Part of our cultural baggage is our hostility to what we often call 'blind obedience' and our preference to conform to laws for which we can see the point. This can affect us and our treatment of the Bible in two subtly different ways.

Thus we may read and interpret what the Bible says and see very clearly that we disagree with it on a particular issue. We may, for example, think a particular statement oppressive or undesirable. Given the value we put on being able to see the point of a law, or to give our consent to it, we may then find it all too easy to think of our non-conformity as being fully justifiable and indeed laudable. The writer C. S. Lewis picks up this kind of thinking in his novel *Perelandra,* which is set on Venus, where a satanic figure tempts a young female of the planet with the thought that this kind of rebellion is both noble and somehow wanted by a god who secretly wishes for us to be 'mature' and 'emancipated', and will 'respect' us for it.

Alternatively, we may find it inconceivable that God would issue a command for which we cannot see the point, and with which, left to ourselves, we would disagree. Accordingly we find ourselves rejecting an interpretation with which we could not agree: 'God could not possibly have meant …' is perhaps the kind of phrase associated with this, where our sense of what is possible comes from our own thinking.

In both these cases there is a resistance to obedience.

For much of the time, however, this resistance may well be hidden from us in our churches precisely because so much of our life as Christians does bear at least some external conformity to what God says, and where we do agree with what the Bible teaches over greed, violence, people-trafficking, lust and similar. Nevertheless, agreement and obedience are distinct, even though they may in a particular situation lead to external actions that look the same: the person who agrees with the prohibition against murder and the person who obeys the prohibition against murder both behave in the same way.

Even so, the difference between obedience and agreement does become visible on those issues where we are clear what the Bible says and we also disagree with it. If, at that point, we change what we believe or do to conform to the Bible, then we obviously are obeying it. This means that a central test for contemporary Christians lies precisely in asking when and how our beliefs and actions have been modified by the Bible in areas where we did not initially agree with it.

There is also a certain quality that goes with this obedience that emerges very clearly in the second temptation. Jesus shows a humility in his relationship with God. This is perhaps implicit in the first temptation, too, as Jesus does not take up Satan's suggestion to satisfy his physical hunger—his status as Son is not to be used for that. But in the second temptation, Jesus' response runs along lines which repudiate any taking of God for granted, or presuming on him. To this extent, Jesus' example can suggest that disobeying God's Word readily goes with attitudes of pride and presumption: we may find it easy to disobey God's Word, because we are proud towards God himself.

Again, this is quite a searching question for Christians in today's churches. We know much about our world, certainly in comparison to previous generations, and are very self-aware of the depth of our knowledge. Do we, then, find it hard to be humble before a text that is thousands of years old in terms of its human authorship? To what extent do we read the Bible humbly? Jesus certainly does seem to read the Bible humbly, and this is connected with another characteristic of his relationship with God's word, his trust.

4. Trust

We can explore Jesus' trust under two main headings, both of which deal with matters of enormous importance: Jesus' inheritance and his resurrection.

a. Trust for inheritance

With regard to the temptation passage from Matthew 4, as well as everything else, Jesus' response to Satan is one of continued trust. Faced with Satan's implied proposal that Jesus look to Satan for the provision of inheritance, Jesus continues to trust his Father, citing his Father's will and aligning himself with his Father as one who continues to trust and believe the promises made in Psalm 2. Jesus trusts his Father will provide the inheritance.

b. Trust for resurrection

Yet Jesus trusts his Father in another profound way too. He goes to the Cross in obedience to his Father's will and dies there, committing his life to his Father (Luke 23:46). In doing so, he is trusting his Father to keep his promise to raise him from the dead, as Peter draws out in his Pentecost speech (Acts 2:27, 31) as he comments on the promise of Psalm 16:10 that God will not allow his holy one to see corruption.

Questions

How could a visitor from the planet Venus tell that we ourselves and our churches think that the Word of God really is a necessity for us, in how we live and how we make decisions?

13

Interpreting the Word of God

Introduction

The last area of Jesus' treatment of God's Word that we must look at is interpretation. Interpretation is not always straightforward. Thus, one of us recently had to sit through a school play which was an adaptation of Shakespeare's tragedy, *Romeo and Juliet*. It was awful, but not because of the children's acting, which was rather good, but because the children had been told to play everything for laughs. Even the deaths and suicides. This was the drama teacher's interpretation and no doubt if we had complained we would have been told it was all just a matter of artistic interpretation. It's a not uncommon assumption: there is no right or wrong to interpretation necessarily. An interpretation may be playful, dynamic, bizarre, counter-intuitive or fun, but we hear evaluations like 'inaccurate', 'distorted', or 'faithful' rather less.

In a similar way there are questions of interpretation about the Bible. Where does interpretation even start?

Can we ever say people are wrong in how they interpret the Bible? Once again, we need to work through how Jesus approaches these questions of interpretation. He must be our model in this as well.

1. The Word of God as cohering around Jesus

For Jesus, God's Word coheres around him. Thus he states in John 5:39 that the Scriptures testify about him. This means that, in order to be able to see how they fit together, we must see them in the light of Jesus. This is carried a stage further as Jesus explains his death and resurrection on two occasions to his disciples in Luke 24, first to the disciples he meets on the road to Emmaus (vv. 26-27) and then to the eleven and their companions in Jerusalem (vv. 44-47). His death and resurrection are fulfilments of what the Old Testament writers promised and, on that basis, repentance and forgiveness of sins are to be preached in Jesus' name to all nations.

This has major consequences. In many ways, interpretation of the Bible begins with realising that it focuses on Jesus. It means we cannot treat the Bible as disjointed, for it finds its centre in Jesus as the fulfilment of God's promises. It means we cannot treat the historical truth of the Bible as irrelevant because the Bible is to do with the fulfilment of God's promises in a particular historical situation. It means we cannot find another centre than Jesus, because that would be to try to make the Bible about something other than what God has intended. It means our interpretations have to be in line with a message of repentance and forgiveness of sins in his name. So an interpretation that purports to be about Jesus but whose agenda is not that of repentance and forgiveness of sins in his name is again not an interpretation that fits with what the Bible is ultimately about. And an interpretation that looks away from all that God fulfilled in Jesus in his life, death and resurrection in the early first century of our era (that does not see, in other words, what God has already done to keep his promises), again does not capture what the Bible is about.

Put this way, Jesus is encouraging us to ask whether how we handle and understand the Bible is faithful to what the Bible is about.

2. The Word of God as capable of being wrongly interpreted

The reason we have to ask whether we have been faithful to the Bible is that Jesus shows us that not all interpretations of the Bible are true. This, again, is quite a challenging thought for us today. We are used to the idea that different opinions can be entertained about what the Bible means. Indeed, one of the factors that contributes to our difficulties in sitting under the Bible is that when there are so many different interpretations, we wonder if it really matters which one we choose.

Again, we need to be clear that this is not how Jesus handles the Bible. He does think some interpretations are just plain wrong. Take Mark 12:18-27 for example. Here Jesus has been challenged with a trick question by the Sadducees, who do not believe in the resurrection and who want to show by their question how absurd the idea is. Jesus' response has several elements to it. He explains both that they are wrong and also why they are wrong.

a. Just plain wrong

First, he tells them repeatedly that they are wrong (vv. 24 and 27). This in itself is shocking enough for a cultural attitude like ours that has stressed the response of the reader to texts, and which can say quite seriously things like, 'If that's what it means to you, then that's what it means.' The Bible is not like a wax nose that can mean whatever a reader thinks, for Jesus tells us emphatically it does not mean what the Sadducees think it means. If we think Jesus is wrong about this, then again the primary issue is not one of biblical interpretation but of who we think Jesus is.

Nor is Jesus apparently impressed by the careful scholarship or sincerity of the Sadducees. They are just plain wrong.

This alters things for us. It is true that some passages of the Bible are hard work to understand and that different people take different views about them. But in view of how Jesus acts here, we cannot respond to this by saying that, when there are so many interpretations, it does not matter which one we pick. Some are wrong, and sincerity does not stop them being wrong. Clearly, some wrong interpretations matter desperately, as does the Sadducees' interpretation here. It is very serious to say resurrection never happens when it does.

So the question that arises for us is whether we still treat getting the right interpretation of a passage in the Bible as something that really matters. We can treat getting the right interpretation as something that doesn't matter when we dismiss a sermon with words like, 'That was just his/her opinion of what the Bible says.' Similarly we treat right interpretation as of secondary importance when we say. 'I've heard that before—nothing fresh.' As preachers and teachers, we start to move away from right interpretation when we are more concerned with saying something striking than saying something true.

b. Why they are wrong

As well as stating that the Sadducees are wrong, Jesus explains why they are wrong, in verse 24. He gives a two-fold reason. The first is that they do not know the Scriptures, and the second is that they do not know the power of God.

Not knowing the Scriptures. With regard to the first, Jesus' criticism is combative. No doubt this is not how the Sadducees would have seen themselves. Jesus' words also have the very obvious application that if we want to understand the Bible correctly, we need to know it extremely well.

At this point we need to face the possibility of a vicious circle in our churches today. As we move away, at least in practice, from the view that the Bible is supremely authoritative to the view that the Bible is one authority amongst several, the incentive to steep ourselves in it becomes less. Indeed, a consistent cry at present is the relative biblical illiteracy amongst today's Christians compared with our forebears. Furthermore, as we know the Bible less well, we will interpret it less well, find it harder and less coherent, and will be even more inclined to see it as only one authority amongst several, and a particularly hard-to-handle authority at that.

We should pick up finally that Jesus' words imply his displeasure at the Sadducees and their biblical ignorance. The sense of what Jesus says is that they should have

known better. More precisely, they should have known
the Bible better.

Not knowing the power of God. The second part of Jesus'
explanation is that the Sadducees do not know the power of God. They have denied that God does or can do
something and have made this denial, it seems, on the
basis of what they think he can do.

This unmasks a profound problem. They have for-
gotten the identity of who is speaking. If it is indeed the
uncreated creator of all speaking, then what he can or
cannot do is emphatically not something that created
humans can work out by themselves on their own. As
creatures, we do not know what it is like to be God, with
an uncreated, perfect and infinite life. We need him to
tell us. This is why Christian theologians have insisted
down the years that God is his own best witness. He
knows himself and us completely and can express himself in terms that are suitable for us and can convey what
he wants conveyed. That will give us not an exhaustive
knowledge of him, but a true knowledge, and a sufficient knowledge for the purposes he intends.

This, of course, takes us right back to why Jesus is
so insistent on the difference between God's Word and
purely human words. Hence, as Jesus underlines that
the Sadducees make their mistake because they do not
know God's power, he is reminding us that we only
know who God is, and what he is like, as we let him
bear witness to himself, and do not imagine that we can
make assumptions about what he 'must' be like, or even
that he must be like what we prefer. When we do make
assumptions of this kind, we are writing God's witness

statement for him. In fact, we are preferring our words and thoughts about him to what he himself has said. This is both a recipe, sadly, for idolatry and also, disturbingly, an indulgence in pride.

Conclusion

As Christians we rightly talk of being more like Christ in daily life. The New Testament frequently encourages us to be imitators of Christ. Throughout this part of the book we have been seeing why and how this applies to the way we treat the Bible.

Crucially, we have seen Jesus draw a distinction between God's Word and purely human words, and we have seen why this follows from who God is and who we are. Accordingly, as imitators of Jesus, we will want to preserve this distinction, too, refusing either to elevate purely human words to the level of God's Word or to downgrade his Word to the level of a purely human word.

We have seen how Jesus treats God's Word: as something necessary, to be obeyed, to be humble before, to trust fully and unreservedly, and as coherent. We have seen him stress the importance of interpreting rightly, and doing this in light of what God shows himself to be rather than what we think he 'must' be.

In all of this, we start to see the limitations of taglines like 'we must read the Bible as any other book'. Yes, we read it using ordinary reading skills and techniques. Yet also, no, because reading 'just like any other book' risks treating its author as 'just like any other author': and he is not. As we have seen, because of who God is, his words are not simply like our words, even if he has chosen to frame them within human languages for the sake of speaking to us. His words are truth, blessing and promise, and it is for that reason that current practices within our churches that tend to devalue God's Word as untruthful, stunting and untrustworthy are such tragic mistakes. Jeremiah prophesied:

> My people have committed two sins:
> they have forsaken me,
>   the spring of living water,
> and have dug their own cisterns,
>   broken cisterns that cannot hold water. (Jer. 2:13)

Sadly, a very effective indicator of forsaking the fountain of living waters is to look for truth and blessing in words coming from others than the real fountain. That is why the current battle for the Bible matters so much: it is a question of whether those who call themselves God's people are in fact only those who worship with their lips and whose hearts are far away, evidenced by the way their treatment of God's Word is the opposite of Jesus's.

Questions

Please think through/discuss the following questions:

- Do you think we have lost the habit of asking whether an interpretation of the Bible is right or wrong?

- Can you think of ways in which we are inclined to dismiss something on the grounds that 'God could not do that'?

CONCLUSION

Who do you Trust?

We started off this short book on the Bible by taking two different perspectives: how the debate about the Bible works when we talk to those who don't believe in Jesus Christ (the 'word for them' section) and how that debate works when we are talking and thinking amongst ourselves who do believe (the 'word for us' section). In fact those two different perspectives are two sides of the same coin—what humans put their faith in. This book is really all about faith and trust.

After all, in the 'word for them' section what kept coming up was the way any human being has faith and trust in something—something that is ultimate for them, something that 'just is'. That may be something outside themselves, a cause like relief for third world debt, or it may simply be themselves, their own intellect or gut instinct. But there is something ultimate in which a human being has faith and trust, and plays that part in how that human being looks at the world and makes judgments.

There again, in the 'word for us' section, what kept coming up was the way a Christian trusts and loves Jesus, and thus trusts and believes him when he talks about the key distinction between the Word of God and purely human words. Here the stress was on the way that a trust and faith in Jesus will treat the Bible in the way he does.

This means that a persistent question for a human being is 'who or what do I have faith in?' The great Genevan theologian of the seventeenth century, Francis Turretin, spoke of 'false faith'. It is a very telling phrase and he applied it to Adam and Eve in Genesis 3. His point was that they had a faith—a trust and final commitment. The trouble was that it was false: false because they believed things about God that were not true, and believed things about themselves that were not true, and indeed things about the serpent that were not true. The tragedy for, and guilt of, those who do not believe in Christ is not that they have no faith, but that they cling to a false faith. Our fear for our churches is that the downgrading of the Bible takes us who want to be Christian more and more towards a false faith.

Turretin makes us think of what counts as true faith as against this false faith. When talking about true, gospel, faith John Calvin spoke of

> a firm and sure knowledge of the divine favour toward us, founded on the truth of a free promise in Christ, and revealed to our minds, and sealed on our hearts, by the Holy Spirit.[1]

---

1   John Calvin, *Institututes of the Christian Religion* III.2.7.

This focuses us once again on Jesus Christ: God freely promises salvation through him. As with any promise, we have to look at who it is who makes the promise and what has actually been promised, not what we wish had been promised or even what we think ought to have been promised, but what actually has been promised. In this respect, as we have seen, Jesus takes us straight back to God's Word, and lives that out himself. To this extent, it turns on Jesus.

It also leaves us with two Jesus-shaped challenges—given that he went to hell and back to make his promise of salvation real:

- The challenge to the world becomes why on Earth do they think they have found someone better to trust than Jesus; and

- The challenge to us is, if we have faith in Jesus and his promises, why not treat God's word in the way that he does.

Going deeper #4
If you want to go even deeper

We hope that this book has built up your own confidence in the Bible as well as your confidence in talking to non-Christians about the Bible. We would love you go on from here and continue having more and more confidence! The first thing to say is that more than anything we want you to be reading the Bible, soaking yourself in it, learning more about the Lord Jesus in it. There is no substitute for regular Bible reading. However, we realise that we have only been able to deal with some issues that people have about the Bible, and then only lightly. Some of you will want to read more, to go into more detail, and to get more technical. We've put together a little list of books we would recommend you to look at. The categories merely show that we've been watching too much *MasterChef* on TV.

1. Other starters to choose from (books a bit like ours!):
Barry Cooper, *Can I Really Trust the Bible?* (The Goodbook Company, 2014). A great little book which covers some of the same material we have covered but is shorter (and probably better written) than ours!

Rich Aldritt and Ash Carter, *God Speaks* (IVP, 2013). Helpful on how God speaks: by his Spirit, through the Bible, about his Son. Both authors are graduates from our college, Oak Hill.

Kevin DeYoung, *Taking God at His Word* (IVP, 2014). Kevin DeYoung has gained a deserved reputation for his writing which is warm, clear and practical. This is a book which unpacks what the Bible says about itself.

2. A good lunch (these will leave you pleasantly full)
J. I. Packer, *Fundamentalism and the Word of God* (Eerdmans, 1958). An absolute classic. Yes, the term 'fundamentalism' has different connotations now, but if you can get over this then Packer's book is a goldmine.

Tim Ward, *Words of Life* (IVP, 2009). Destined to become a classic. Tim is Associate Director of the Cornhill Training Course in London. A brilliant restatement of an orthodox view of Scripture which is aware of the deep theological and philosophical issues that have been swirling around for decades. Arguably one of the best books on the Bible in the last decade.

Vishal Mangalwadi, *The Book that Made Your World* (Thomas Nelson, 2011). We've already mentioned this one. Mangalwadi is an Indian scholar. The book charts the impact of the Bible on Western civilization.

3. The Sunday roast with all the trimmings (Get stuffed!)
John Frame, *Doctrine of the Word of God* (P&R, 2010). Yes, it's getting on for 700 pages, but, as with all Frame, it's very readable and for a more meaty read does not suffer from academic diarrhoea. Comprehensive, creative and pretty compelling on everything to do with the doctrines of revelation and Scripture.

Craig Blomberg, *The Historical Reliability of the Gospels* (IVP, 2007). Blomberg is a well established figure when it comes to writing about biblical reliability. A really helpful resource for those wanting to read more about the Bible and history.

James Hoffmaier and Dennis Magary, *Do Historical Matters Matter to Faith?* (Crossway, 2012). A new collection of contemporary essays on the Bible and history by a group of biblical scholars who all defend an orthodox view of Scripture without wanting to duck the hard questions.

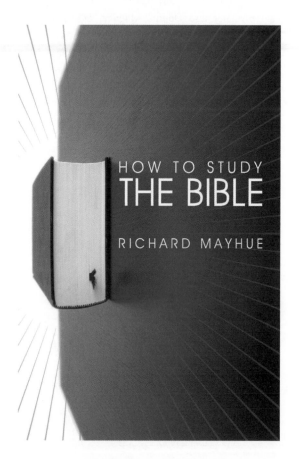

HOW TO STUDY
THE BIBLE

RICHARD MAYHUE

How to Study the Bible
by Richard Mayhue

Richard Mayhue provides tools to enrich your study
time by understanding what the Bible says and means
through methods of Biblical interpretation. His study
tips will guide you to avoid common errors and to find
a straight path to understanding the Truth of Scriptures
for yourself.

ISBN: 978-1-84550-203-4

taking the
BIBLE
at its
WORD

PAUL WELLS

Taking the Bible at its Word
by Paul Wells

God's Word is the same yesterday, today and forever! God's Complete Word still speaks to us today. It tells the story of God coming to us for our salvation. We are given the possibility to know God and what he did for us. We can find no way to climb up to God. Our only hope lies in movement from the other direction-God coming down to us. The Bible shows a God who reveals himself to his people in the Old Testament and by the coming of Jesus Christ in the New Testament.

ISBN: 978-1-84550-969-9

STEVE LEVY
WITH PAUL BLACKHAM

FOREWORD BY
RICHARD BEWES

BIBLE
OVERVIEW

Bible Overview
by Steve Levy and Paul Blackham

Foreword by Richard Bewes: This will give you a brilliant introduction to the Bible! Written with young people and new believers in mind, Steve helps us get to grips with the structure and the meaning of God's Word. In fact it is Steve's desire that we delight after God's Word and he hopes that desire to devour God's Word and enjoy it would be birthed in us. The group study material from each chapter is available to download.

ISBN: 978-1-84550-378-9

If God is Triune, Do Christians Believe in Three Gods? p.15
Can God Create a Rock so Big That He Can't Pick It Up? p.25
Is God Guilty of Genocide? p.35
How Did Jesus Perform His Miracles? p.46
Did Jesus Descend into Hell? p.63
Can a Christian Commit the Sin unto Death? p.77
Is Suicide the Unpardonable Sin? p.91
Are All World Religions Pathways to the Same God? p.99
Do Atheists Actually Believe in God After All? p.111

TOUGH TOPICS2

Biblical answers to
25 challenging questions

Can All Christians Pray for God to Save the Lost? p.117
Is Water Baptism Necessary for Salvation? p.133
Does Hell Last Forever? p.151
Will the Horror of Hell Spoil the Happiness of Heaven? p.165
Did Joshua Really Make the Sun Stand Still? p.181
Does Paul Restrict the Office of Elder and Senior Pastor to Men? p.195
What Did Jesus Teach about Divorce and Remarriage? p.211
What Did Paul Teach about Divorce and Remarriage? p.223
Can a Divorced Man Serve as an Elder in the Local Church? p.239
Is It Ever OK for a Christian to Swear an Oath (or to Lie)? p.245
Does the Bible Endorse Capital Punishment? p.257
Does Prayer Really Change Things? p.271
Is the Man in Romans 7 a Christian or a Non-Christian? p.289
What Does It Mean to Forgive Someone as God Has Forgiven Me? p.309
What Did Jesus Mean When He Said 'Turn the Other Cheek'
and 'Love Your Enemies'? p.329
What is the Meaning of '666'? p.341

SAM STORMS

Tough Topics 2
by Sam Storms

Countless people are worried, angry, fearful and just plain confused when it comes to some of the more perplexing issues that life poses and the Bible provokes. Tough Topics 2 provides solid and scriptural answers to 25 such questions. Sam Storms seeks to tackle frustration by looking deeply, not superficially, at what Scripture says, deriving clear and persuasive explanations for these thorny matters.

ISBN: 978-1-78191-552-3

Christian Focus Publications

Our mission statement –

STAYING FAITHFUL

In dependence upon God we seek to impact the world through literature faithful to His infallible Word, the Bible. Our aim is to ensure that the Lord Jesus Christ is presented as the only hope to obtain forgiveness of sin, live a useful life and look forward to heaven with Him.

Our books are published in four imprints:

CHRISTIAN
FOCUS

Popular works including bi-ographies, commentaries, basic doctrine and Christian living.

CHRISTIAN
HERITAGE

Books representing some of the best material from the rich heritage of the church.

MENTOR

Books written at a level suitable for Bible College and seminary students, pastors, and other serious readers. The imprint in-cludes commentaries, doctrinal studies, examination of current issues and church history.

CF4•K

Children's books for quality Bible teaching and for all age groups: Sunday school curriculum, puzzle and activity books; personal and family devotional titles, biographies and inspirational stories – because you are never too young to know Jesus!

Christian Focus Publications Ltd,
Geanies House, Fearn, Ross-shire,
IV20 1TW, Scotland, United Kingdom.
www.christianfocus.com
blog.christianfocus.com